MARINE CORPS HISTORICAL REFERENCE PAMPHLET

A Brief History of the 2d Marines

Revised by

Captain Robert J. Kane, USMC

First Printing: 1961
Revised: 1962
Revised: 1969

Historical Division
Headquarters, U. S. Marine Corps
Washington, D. C. 20380
1970

MARINE CORPS

JAN 26 1971

REFERENCE BRANCH

15554

PREFACE

"A Brief History of the 2d Marines" is a concise narrative of regiments bearing the designation "2d" prior to 1913, and of the 2d Marines since its initial organization over a half-century ago. Official records and an update of appropriate historical works were used in compiling this revised chronicle. It is published for the information of those interested in events in which the 2d Marines have participated.

W. J. VAN RYZIN
Lieutenant General, U. S. Marine Corps
Chief of Staff

Reviewed and approved: 8 October 1970

TABLE OF CONTENTS

Preface... i

SECTION I
  The Provisional Regiments......................... 1

SECTION II
  The 2d Marines.................................... 5

SECTION III
  The War Years....................................14

SECTION IV
  Decade by Decade.................................29

Reading List..37

Appendixes:

  A. Footnotes......................................41
  B. Commanding Officers, 2d Marines...............47
  C. Chronology, Provisional Regiments.............53
  D. Chronology, 2d Marines........................54
  E. Honors of the 2d Marines......................56
  F. Medal of Honor Recipients.....................58

SECTION I

The Provisional Regiments

The first "2d Regiment" of Marines came into existence early in 1901 when unsettled conditions in the Far East required the presence of a Marine expeditionary force to protect American lives and property. The regiment was formed at Cavite, Philippine Islands on 1 January(1), by utilizing personnel from units recently returned to the Philippines from service during the Boxer Rebellion in China, namely, the 1st Regiment and the 4th and 5th Independent Battalions. The 2d Regiment, under the command of Lieutenant Colonel Allen C. Kelton, became part of the 1st Brigade of Marines stationed in the Philippines as a ready force to be committed wherever needed in Far Eastern Waters.(2) Following the collapse of the Philippine Insurrection, the 2d was given an additional mission of helping carry out United States Navy responsibilities for the military government of Cavite Peninsula and the Subic Bay area.

The Marines of the regiment established garrisons and outposts, and continually patrolled their assigned areas with an objective of capturing the remaining insurgents and maintaining law and order. In order to execute the regiment's military government responsibilities, officers were appointed to special duties such as captains of the ports, district commanders, inspectors of customs, internal revenue collectors, and provost judges and marshals. As the political situation in the Philippines returned to normalcy, drill, practice marches, and general field training were emphasized to a greater degree.(3)

Company F of the 2d was part of a provisional battalion sent from Cavite, on 20 October 1901, to the island of Samar (in the southern Philippines) to reinforce and cooperate with United States Army troops in operations against insurgents on the island.(4) The Samar episode was one of the last guerrilla actions that occurred during the Philippine Insurrection. By April 1902, the 1st Brigade was primarily regarded as a force-in-readiness for employment anywhere in the Asiatic area.(5) To increase the effectiveness of such expeditionary forces, the Navy Department provided necessary logistical materiel at Cavite to be used in seizing and defending a forward base.(6)

Early in 1903, the 2d Regiment provided personnel for an expeditionary force of 200 Marines, accompanied by materiel (ammunition and equipment) from the advance base depot, which participated in a Navy advance base exercise. The Marines were to seize an undefended harbor on a hypothetical enemy coast and then defend it against invading hostile forces. The Marine force occupied Grande Island, at the entrance of Subic Bay, and mounted guns for the protection of minefields in the channels on either side of the island.

After the maneuvers had been completed, the regiment, on 5 February, provided troops for an expeditionary force of 500 men established at Olongapo to hold itself in readiness for possible future employment.(7) At this time, the bulk of the regiment moved from Cavite to Olongapo, with only one company remaining at Cavite.

The 2d continued its garrison and patrol duties during its later years in the Philippines. Routine training life in the area was from time to time interrupted by minor clashes with bandits. Marine details were frequently provided for shipboard duty in Asiatic waters, with the ships' detachments sometimes being employed ashore to protect American interests.(8) In December 1911, for instance, Companies B and C were aboard the USS Rainbow cruising off the China coast, while, at the same time, Company E was assigned ashore at Peking. In August 1912, Company A rotated for its turn of duty on the Rainbow.(9)

In January of 1914, the regiment reassigned most of its units to ships and other stations in the Far East. With the transfer of the Field and Staff (Headquarters) to the Provisional Regiment, Guam on 20 January, the 2d Regiment was formally disbanded. Although Company A was left at Peking, Company B at Cavite, and Company D at Olongapo, these companies ceased to carry "2d Regiment" as part of their designation.(10)

Prior to 1913, there were a number of temporary organizations in the Marine Corps created for specific purposes or tasks and designated as regiments. However, when a particular unit was no longer needed (its purpose or task completed) it was generally disbanded and the attached companies returned to their original stations. It was not uncommon for the Marine Corps to have two or more regiments bearing the same designation. Consequently, at the same time a "2d Regiment" was serving in the Far East, the 2d Regiment, 1st Provisional Brigade consisting of a Field and Staff, and Companies A, B, C, and F was organized at League Island, Pennsylvania on 26 December 1903.(11) The regiment embarked and sailed this same date to Panama arriving there on 3 January 1904.

The primary mission of this force in Panama was the enforcement of provisions of the Hay-Herran Treaty made with Panama on 18 November 1903 which provided for the construction of a cross-isthmus canal. The treaty provided that any and all operations by the United States would be designed to ensure a stable government in that republic, to safeguard the construction of the canal, and the operation of the railroad.(12)

The 2d Regiment, commanded by Lieutenant Colonel Littleton W. T. Waller, aided in establishing and maintaining peace and order in the republic. The Marines gained considerable knowledge of the country while on reconnaissance to make studies for defense of both the canal and city of Panama.(13) On 14 February 1904, with the regiment's mission accomplished, the 2d was disbanded at Panama and personnel were utilized to form separate battalions, one of which relocated to Guantanamo Bay, Cuba for duty.(14)

A revolution broke out in Cuba in late 1906, and a Marine expeditionary force was dispatched to the island to establish and maintain law and order.(15) As part of this force, the 4th Expeditionary Battalion was formed at League Island, Pennsylvania on 27 September 1906.(16) With Lieutenant Colonel Franklin J. Moses in command, the battalion sailed for Cuba, arriving at Camp Columbia on 8 October. Here it was reorganized and redesignated as the 2d Regiment, 1st Expeditionary Brigade.(17) Order was soon restored, and upon the arrival of United States Army troops as occupation forces on 31 October, the 2d Regiment was disbanded. The major portion of its personnel were assigned to the newly created 1st Provisional Regiment stationed in Cuba for duty with Army forces.

The 2d Expeditionary Regiment was formed at Philadelphia in mid-December 1909,(18) to assist in maintaining order in Panama during the republic's elections that year. The regiment, with Colonel Eli K. Cole commanding, departed from Philadelphia on 14 December arriving in the Canal Zone several days later. The 2d remained in the Republic of Panama until 13 April 1910, when 200 of its Marines boarded the USS Buffalo for Mare Island, California. The following day, the bulk of the regiment again embarked on the Prairie for the return trip to Philadelphia, where it arrived on 25 April and disbanded.(19)

On 9 March 1911, yet another "2d" was formed at Philadelphia. This 2d Regiment, 1st Provisional Brigade was designed for duty in Cuba because of internal disorder which threatened United States interests.(20) The men of the 2d boarded the USS Dixie on 9 and 11 March and sailed for Guantanamo arriving the 15th. Within three months, order was restored on the island, and in June, the 2d returned to the United States where it was disbanded at Philadelphia on the 14th.(21)

In the spring of 1912, revolt again flared in Cuba, and Marines were once more called to the island. On 27 May, the 2d Provisional Regiment was formed at Philadelphia and Norfolk(22) to reinforce the 1st Provisional Regiment already in Cuba. Under command of Colonel James E. Mahoney, the 2d Regiment sailed in several Navy vessels for Cuba, where Companies B, D, and E helped quell the revolt. Within two months, peace again prevailed in the island, and on 1 August the 2d Provisional Regiment was deactivated and its personnel transferred to the newly reorganized 1st Provisional Regiment in Cuba or returned to the United States.(23)

Revolution occurred in the Dominican Republic in 1911 and 1912, resulting in the customs service being interrupted, particularly along the Haitian border, where the rebels captured and held several forts. To avert further trouble, the United States sent two commissioners to the republic to look into violations of the 1907 treaty, which provided for the collection of customs by United States agents.(24) These commissioners were backed up by the 2d Provisional Regiment, commanded by Colonel Franklin J. Moses. Formed at Philadelphia on 27 September 1912(25) and comprising Companies A through F, the regiment arrived off Santo Domingo City on 2 October. For the next two months, the Marines of the regiment remained onboard the Prairie as she patrolled the waters off the city while negotiations progressed. On 1 December, after a peaceful settlement had been reached between revolutionary factions in the republic, the regiment set sail for the United States, disbanding when it arrived at Philadelphia on the 7th.(26)

The final one of these temporary "2d Regiment" organizations to be formed was designated as the 2d Regiment, 2d Provisional Brigade on 19 February 1913 at Philadelphia.(27) Headed by Colonel Joseph H. Pendleton, the regiment was originally intended for duty in Mexico as part of an expeditionary brigade. Instead, it was sent to Guantanamo Bay and held in readiness for emergency duties there, while undergoing intensive training. On 1 May, this unit was redesignated 2d Regiment, Expeditionary Force, USMC.(28) As such, it remained in Cuba until the latter part of the month, when it boarded the Prairie for the United States, arriving at Philadelphia on 1 June, when it was dissolved.(29)

SECTION II

The 2d Marines

The lineage of the present day 2d Marines can be traced back to the activation of the 1st Advance Base Regiment at Philadelphia on 19 June 1913.(30) This regiment was composed of C Company, a mine company trained to handle harbor defense mines; E Company, a signal company trained in radio, telephone, telegraph, buzzers, and visual signalling; a field artillery battery which manned 3-inch field pieces; F and I Companies with responsibilities for fixed batteries to be mounted in harbor defense; and H Company which was trained both as an engineer company and as a machine gun company. The regiment was to provide the force of technical troops and equipment required for the seizure and defense of an advance base. In the beginning, the 1st Advance Base Regiment was generally referred to as the "Fixed Defense Regiment." However, each company was also thoroughly schooled in infantry weapons and tactics to ensure that all Marines were thoroughly familiar with their primary occupational specialty.

On 23 December 1913, this same regiment became part of the Advance Base Brigade formed at Philadelphia.(31) On 3 January 1914, it sailed with the brigade for maneuvers with the Atlantic Fleet at Culebra, Puerto Rico. These maneuvers, forerunners of many to come over the years, consisted of the occupation and defense of the island of Culebra by the Advance Base Brigade, with the landing force of the Atlantic Fleet acting as aggressor forces. The mission of the 1st Regiment, in defense, included emplacement of batteries of 3-inch guns on each side of the entrance to Culebra's harbor and the laying of control mines offshore. The signal company, in addition to laying mines, provided communications (telegraph and telephone) for the brigade, established radio stations, and operated day and night visual stations. The engineers assisted the fixed gun companies in the preparation of gun emplacements, built docks, and established machine gun positions on certain parts of the harbor shore line. The 1st 3-inch battery emplaced 4.7-inch guns in permanent positions, holding its 3-inch field pieces in reserve.

Upon the successful completion of these maneuvers, the regiment sailed to Pensacola, Florida and then on to New Orleans, Louisiana. Here, on 18 February 1914, the 1st Advance Base Regiment was redesignated 1st Regiment, Advance Base Brigade.(32) For the next two months, under command of Lieutenant Colonel Charles G. Long, the regiment operated onboard ship off New Orleans and Algiers, Louisiana.

The location of the regiment at this time was no accident; its operation in waters just north of Mexico was part of another

First Marine Landing Party leaves USS Prairie at Vera Cruz, 21Apr14. (USMC Photo #521570)

Marines at Vera Cruz, Mexico 1914. (USMC Photo #514627)

show of force by the United States in protest of the rule of the latest revolutionary victor in that country.(33) The Mexican situation worsened, and Marine forces were ordered to land at Vera Cruz in response to an insult to the American Flag, in order to seize the customs house and prevent the landing of arms and ammunition by belligerents. The 1st Regiment landed on 22 April and joined other forces in clearing the city.(34) Sectors of Vera Cruz were assigned to each regiment with orders to search every building for arms, to arrest all suspicious persons, and to prevent snipers from operating. The search, hampered by continuous sniping, was exhausting and difficult. On the 23d, opposition slackened with the Marines occupying a large area of the city. On 30 April, United States Army forces moved in with the Marine Advance Base Brigade. The 1st Regiment took its turn at outpost duty and used the opportunity for field training. On 23 November, its Mexican tasks completed, the regiment returned to Philadelphia.(35)

On 3 December, the entire brigade was reorganized with one regiment given the mission of fixed defense and the other, that of mobile defense. The 1st Regiment, the fixed defense regiment, was assigned a fire control unit and eight companies. These included four 5-inch gun companies, a searchlight company, a mine company, an engineer company, and an anti-aircraft company. (36) The increase of firepower inherent in this reorganization strengthened the regiment's capabilities in keeping with Navy interests for the further development of the Marine Advance Base Force.

By the summer of 1915, however, it became necessary to put aside advance base work for immediate problems. This time, the 1st Regiment, headed by Colonel Theodore P. Kane was called to reinforce Marine forces in Haiti. The policy which dictated United States intervention resulted from requests by American business interests and the chaotic conditions which then existed in Haiti. Also, the United States felt obligated by the Monroe Doctrine to protect the interests and property of foreign (European) nations.(37)

On 15 August, the 1st Regiment, minus the 2d Company which remained at Philadelphia for instruction in submarine mining, landed the 4th, 6th, and 22d Companies at Port au Prince and the 5th, 11th, 19th, and 23d Companies at Cape Haitien.(38)

In addition to rendering assistance in maintaining the economic stability of the country, the regiment carried out extensive patrolling into the interior of the country. An estimated 25,000 to 50,000 Cacos lived in the rugged mountains contiguous with the Dominican Republic. These people were soldiers of fortune who lived on the country as bandits in normal times and supported one or the other of the candidates for the presidency during revolutionary periods. The mission of the 1st Regiment in the next few months was to seek out and

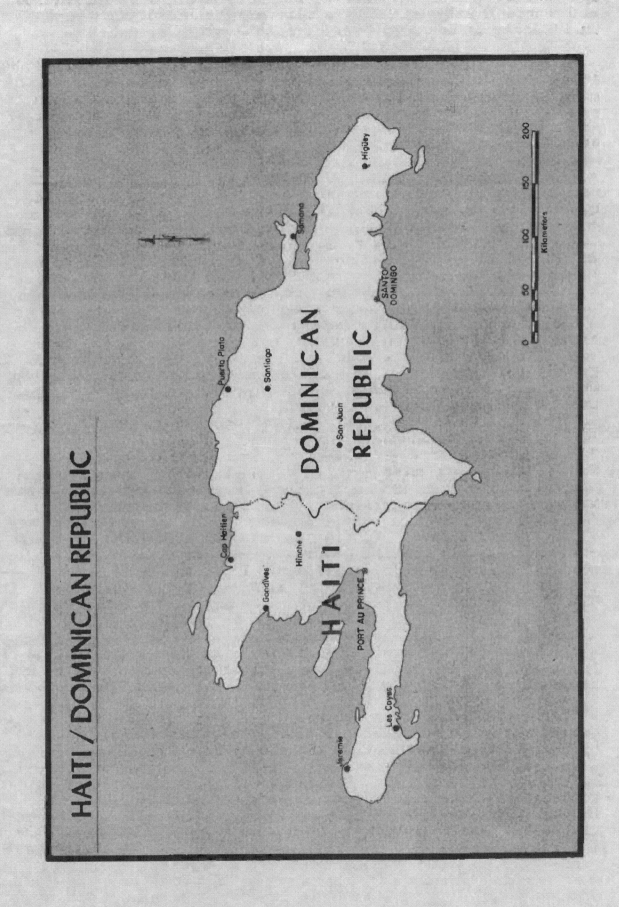

appease, or "tame" the Cacos. The Marines had many skirmishes with these rebels, with the attack and capture of Fort Riviere on 17 November being an engagement of particular note.

The fort was situated on the summit of Montagne Noir, 4,000 feet above the sea, which commanded the surrounding country for miles in every direction. The fort itself was an old French bastion of approximately 200 square feet with thick walls of brick and stone. The walls had been loopholed to command the plain at the foot of the height.

All avenues of approach had been previously closed so that no Cacos could escape. The only real difficulty encountered by the Marines, was in crossing an open plain 800 yards wide under heavy fire. Fortunately for the Marines, the fire of the Cacos was inaccurate. One company of Marines advanced while covering fire was provided by two other companies. The main entrance to the fort on the north had been sealed by the Cacos and a breach in the south wall had been made for passage. It was through this hole that the Marines forced their way, overwhelming the enemy within the fort in a vicious 10-minute, hand-to-hand fray which resulted in a total of 51 Cacos being killed, including their leader General Joseph Dorzeme Michels. The Marines suffered no casualties. The forces involved in the attack on Fort Riviere were the 5th Company (Captain W. W. Low), the 13th Company (Captain C. Campbell), Marine Detachment, Connecticut (Captain Barker), Seaman Company, Connecticut (Lt (jg) S. D. Mc Caughey) and Automatic Gun Detachment, 3d Company. The actual assault on the fort was made by the 5th Company which accounted for 29 of the 51 Cacos. The remaining 22 jumped from the fort during the hand-to-hand combat and were killed by the covering forces.

With the capture of Fort Capois shortly thereafter, Haiti became relatively stable and its inhabitants resumed more peaceful pursuits. The regiment continued to patrol and garrison a number of towns until called to the neighboring Dominican Republic where internal disorder in the early months of 1916 threatened American lives and property.

By the end of April, the 1st Regiment had joined the 1st, 9th, 13th (artillery), 14th, and 24th Companies from the 2d Regiment in Haiti, and in the early part of May, these companies, together with the 4th, 5th, 6th, and 19th Companies of the regiment were moved to Santo Domingo City to protect the American Legation and later to occupy the city during a period of insurrection. On 1 July, the companies remaining in Haiti were detached from the 1st Regiment. On this same date, the 1st Regiment was redesignated the 2d Regiment and vice versa. Consequently, the 1st Regiment, which was in Haiti, was then, through redesignation, the 2d Regiment. All lineage and honors of the old 1st Regiment than belonged to the 2d Regiment. On 1 July the 2d Regiment was comprised of Field and Staff, Naval

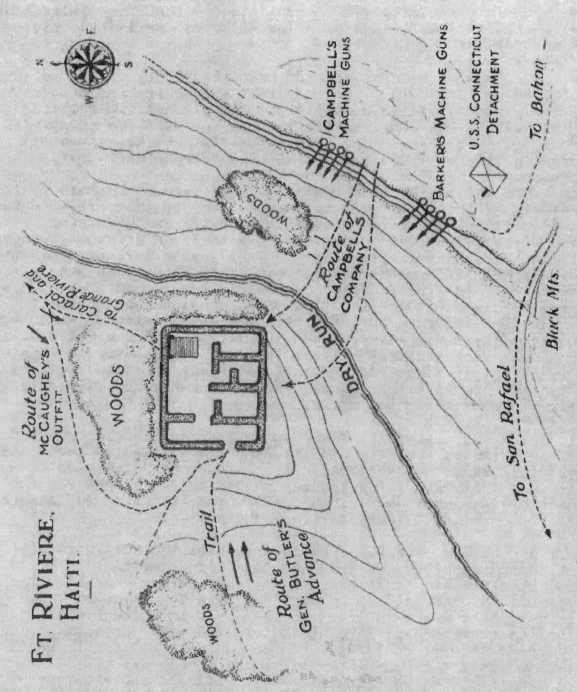

Capture of Fort Riviere. (USMC Photo #522218)

Detachment, 1st and 2d Sections of the 7th and 17th Companies, and the 15th, 16th, 20th, and 23d Companies. The 11th, 19th, and 22d Companies joined the 2d during July and the 18th Company joined on 8 September.(39) The 11th Company went on an expedition to the Dominican Republic late in July to seek arms of the revolutionists while the remaining companies remained with the 2d in Haiti. By the end of the summer, bandit activity had quieted down and the regiment settled into a more normal routine. Although some patrolling continued, the main activity centered around training the Marines of the 2d and the men of the newly organized Haitian Constabulary.(40)

The 15th Company of the regiment formed part of a mounted expedition sent to Azua, Dominican Republic, in September to quell a rebellion. On 12 November, its range firing completed, the 10th Company rejoined the regiment and was stationed at Fortaleza de San Luis, Santiago, Dominican Republic.(41)

When the decrease in bandit activity and the active participation of the United States during 1917 and 1918 in World War I, the frustrated 2d Regiment spent the war years in routine barracks duty. Occasional patrol activity and frequent changes in organization and personnel did little to alleviate the disappointment of those Marines stuck in the tropics and who were not able to take part in the great war. In the early months of 1917, the 53d, 54th, and 57th Companies joined the regiment and the 7th, 11th, 17th, 20th, and 22d Companies were detached. Later that spring, the 2d began to benefit from the war mobilization efforts of the United States. When the 16th and 23d Companies were detached on 25 May, sufficient personnel were available to organize the 64th and 65th Companies. The only notable events of the next year and a half were the frequent changes of command.

The spring of 1919, however, witnessed a considerable increase in bandit activity in Haiti. On 26 March, the 36th, 100th, 148th, and 153d Companies joined the regiment, and a month later, the 2d took to the field as the native gendarmerie was unable to contain the increasing banditry. Four of the regiment's companies operated in southern Haiti, while two companies moved into the rural areas in the central part of the island. During the month of May, all companies of the 2d Regiment, except the 148th, participated in a concerted drive to clear the republic of thieves and bandits. The 196th and 197th Companies joined the 2d in June, and both companies assisted in mopping up the bandit strongholds during the following several months.

On 17 December, the 36th, 57th, 63d, 100th, 148th, and 196th Companies were transferred to the 8th Regiment.(42) With the organization of the Supply Company on 24 January 1920, the 2d Regiment was composed of Field and Staff, Supply, 53d, 54th, 62d, 64th, 153d, and 197th Companies.(43) The Field and Staff

Marines in search of bandits in Haiti, 1919. (USMC Photo #519898)

2d Regiment in formation at MB, Port-au-Prince, Haiti, 22 Feb 1932. (USMC Photo #515035)

was redesignated Headquarters Company on 1 February.

During 1920-21, with banditry finally suppressed and peace restored, the regiment continued its garrison duties with reduced personnel, assisting in the training of the native constabulary and performing other duties incident to the occupation.(44)

The years 1922-1929 were peaceful ones for the Marines of the 2d Regiment as Haiti remained quiet, with considerable progress being made in sociological and technological areas in the country. Patrolling and mapping continued as the regiment increased its knowledge of Haiti and its ways. At this same time, Marines of the 2d Regiment were thoroughly indoctrinated on how to deal with the natives. Military training occupied most of the 2d's time with frequent exercises being held.(45)

Changes in the command and organization of the regiment continued throughout the next two years. On 1 July 1924, Headquarters Company, Service Company (formerly Supply Company), and the 62d Company (recently rejoined) were reorganized.(46) Headquarters and the 62d Companies were combined into a new Headquarters Company on 3 June 1925.(47) When the 8th Regiment was disbanded in Haiti on 1 July, its Headquarters, 100th, 63d, and 64th Companies joined the 2d Regiment.(48) Headquarters Company of the 2d Regiment was redesignated Headquarters and Headquarters Company, 2d Battalion, 2d Regiment. Headquarters and the 100th Companies from the 8th Regiment were combined and designated Headquarters and Headquarters Company, 2d Regiment, 1st Brigade. On this same date, the 26th, 54th, and 53d (Machine Gun) Companies joined the 2d Regiment. As a result of these changes, the regiment, as of 1 July, was composed of Headquarters and Headquarters Company, 36th, 53d (Machine Gun), 63d, and 64th Companies stationed at Port-au-Prince. The 2d Battalion, composed of Headquarters and Headquarters Company, and the 54th Company, was stationed at Camp Haitien. On 1 March 1926, the 63d Company was transferred to the 2d Battalion, relieving the 54th Company, which joined the 2d Regiment at Port-au-Prince.(49)

In the fall of 1926, Marines of the regiment assisted in quelling political disturbances in Haiti, but most of the 2d's occupational activity was turned to improving the lot of the natives and developing natural resources on the island. During these latter years of its Haitian tour, the regiment assisted in building roads and schools, improving sanitary conditions, and training and supervising the native constabulary.

On 1 January 1933, as part of a Marine Corps-wide redesignation of units, the 2d Regiment was redesignated 2d Marines, its present and permanent designation.(50) On the same date, the 36th and 54th Companies were disbanded, and the 53d, 63d, and 64th Companies were redesignated Companies D, B, and C respectively.

Companies C and D were transferred to the United States on 26 July 1934, and on 8 August, Company B was disbanded. With evacuation of the 1st Brigade from Haiti, Headquarters Company of the 2d was dissolved on 15 August 1934, and the 2d Marines disappeared from the official records for nearly seven years.(51)

SECTION III

The War Years

The 2d Marines, commanded by Colonel Joseph C. Fegan, was officially reactivated as part of the 2d Marine Division at Marine Corps Base, San Diego on 1 February 1941.(52) In April, the regiment moved to Camp Elliott, San Diego and began intensive training in the mechanics of amphibious warfare.

The Japanese attack on Pearl Harbor in December 1941 caused some apprehension that the enemy might attack our West Coast. The 2d Marines was alerted to assist in protecting the area from Oceanside to the Mexican border.(53) When the danger of immediate invasion abated, the 2d returned to Camp Elliott to assist in training recruits. The 2d Marines was redesignated 2d Marines (Reinforced) (54) during May 1942 while its units were training in the San Diego area.

As part of a larger force, the 2d Marines (Reinforced), embarked and sailed from San Diego on 1 July 1942, arriving in the Transport Area off Koro Island on the 25th in sufficient time to take part in the final rehearsal prior to the Guadalcanal operations.(55) The 2d was in reserve for this operation, and yet provided the first Marines to land.

On 7 August, prior to the main assault on Guadalcanal by the 1st Marine Division, Company B (Reinforced), 2d Marines landed on Florida Island to protect the left flank of the Marines executing the Tulagi landing.(56) While Company B and its reinforcing elements deployed inland, the remainder of the 1st Battalion landed on Florida, near Gavutu and Tanambogo. By early afternoon, it had cleared its objective and reembarked to await further orders. Company B meanwhile, was ordered to assist the 1st Parachute Battalion in clearing Tanambogo, but because of the intensity of enemy fire, it was forced to withdraw to the transport area.

On the following morning, the 3d Battalion, 2d Marines landed on Gavutu Island and assisted the 1st Parachute Battalion in clearing Tanambogo on 9 August. The other two infantry battalions of the regiment landed on Tulagi on the 9th, and by that evening, had secured the small islands of the Tulagi area. Subsequent operations in that area consisted of mopping up and consolidating positions.

The 3d Battalion, 2d Marines, was moved from Tulagi to Guadalcanal on 14 September and inserted in the east side of the perimeter between elements of the 5th and 7th Marines.(57) It continued to man that position until early in October, when it

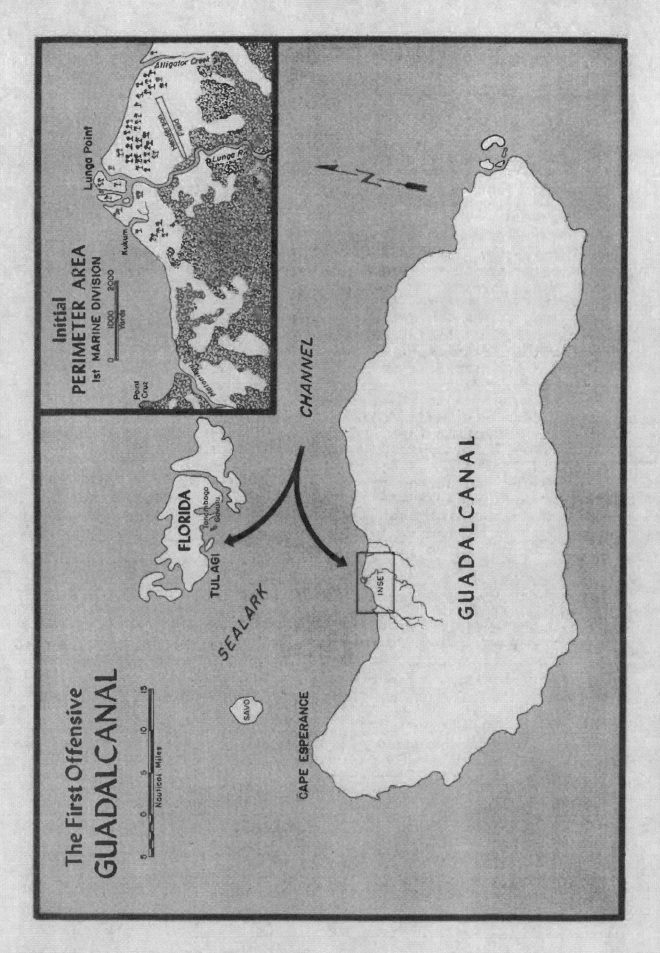

participated in the Matanikau Offensive from the 7th to the 9th. The battalion then became part of the 1st Marine Division reserve once more and remained in that capacity until the 30th, when it returned to Tulagi for garrison duty and a well earned rest.

Meanwhile, elements of the 2d Battalion, 2d Marines, raided the area near the village of Koilotumaria and Garabusu, Guadalcanal, on 10 October, and returned to Tulagi two days later.(58) The 1st and 2d Battalions patrolled the Tulagi area until the 28th, consolidating positions off the coast of Florida.

The 2d Marines (-) moved to Guadalcanal on the 29th to participate, as part of a larger force, in the push towards Kokumbona. When the Japanese again threatened in the Koli Point area, the Kokumbona drive was terminated, and the two battalions of the 2d were assigned defensive positions in the Point Cruz area. The regiment, as part of a larger force, again moved forward on 10 November, to regain most of the ground given up earlier in the month, when the division had been forced to shift its attention eastward.

During the next six weeks, the 2d Marines was shifted about within the Guadalcanal perimeter, reinforcing danger spots and consolidating defensive positions along the front lines. On 12 January 1943, the regiment relieved the 1st Battalion, 8th Marines to participate, as part of XIV Corps, in offensive operations to the west of Point Cruz. Two days later, the 2d Marines was relieved and returned to a reserve area preparatory to leaving the island.

After rejoining its 3d Battalion from Tulagi, it left Guadalcanal on 31 January and sailed for New Zealand, arriving at Wellington on 6 February.(59) Here, as part of the 2d Marine Division, the regiment rested, reorganized, and trained for nearly a year. Liberty and leave were granted liberally, so that all Marines had an opportunity to see New Zealand and to become acquainted with its hospitable people. A well planned recreation program was implemented. But training went on, too, with the transition from play to work being brought about gradually.

The 2d Marine Division, including the 2d Marines, was attached to V Amphibious Corps on 15 September.(60) The Marines of the regiment attended various specialist schools, such as tank, intelligence, etc., and then made good use of their added instruction in the execution of amphibious training exercises.

The regiment sailed on 28 October, as part of the 2d Marine Division, for Efate, south of Espiritu Santo, to take part in final rehearsals for the landing at Tarawa.(61) At Efate, on 7 November, Colonel Marshall, who had rebuilt the 2d Marines in New Zealand, became ill and had to be returned to the United States. The following day, Lieutenant Colonel David M. Shoup

Patrol on Guadalcanal, August 1942. (USMC Photo #50831)

Assault on Tarawa, November 1943. (USMC Photo #63909)

(22d Commandant of the Marine Corps, 1960-1963), the division's operations officer, received a spot-promotion to colonel and was assigned the command of the regiment.(62)

The 2d Marines (Reinforced), with the 2d Battalion, 8th Marines attached, assaulted Betio Island, the main defensive bastion of the Japanese positions on Tarawa Atoll, on the morning of 20 November. Just prior to the main landing, the Scout-Sniper Platoon, H&S Company, 2d Marines, arrived at the end of the long pier jutting into the sea and proceeded to clear it of enemy forces. This helped the main assault forces move in towards their assigned beaches, but the Japanese fire was still murderous. Only the first three waves of Marines were mounted in amphibian tractors, which enabled them to cross the fringe coral reef and move steadily to the shore. The later waves were composed of landing craft, none of which could traverse the barrier reef. The Marines in these craft got out as best they could, stumbled across the reef, and waded towards shore. The toll in Marine blood was a costly price exacted by the devastating fire from well integrated gun positions on the island. These later waves kept the attack moving and helped defend the beachhead won by the assault waves.

In the latter part of the morning, Colonel Shoup and his staff landed and set up a command post on the pier, and, later, on the beach. With the situation in critical balance, Colonel Shoup committed his reserve in the afternoon. By nightfall, Combat Team 2 (the name given the assault force) was clinging precariously to a slim perimeter and subject to continuous heavy enemy fire.

Early the following morning, reinforced by the remainder of the 8th Marines, Combat Team 2 pushed inland. Progress was slow and casualties were high. But elements of the 1st and 2d Battalions, 2d Marines, supported by the 1st Battalions, 10th Marines, naval gunfire, and two tanks, managed to struggle southward to secure Green Beach, from which the anti-boat guns had been pouring death and destruction on the Marines still attempting to land.(63) In the afternoon, the situation turned to Marine advantage, as more room became available to land and maneuver. By nightfall, the 6th Marines began to land, and on arrival, the entire 2d Marine Division was committed. The attack was continued on the 22d with the Marines of the regiment holding their hard-won gains against vicious counter-attacks. That night, the 1st Battalion, 2d Marines, helped repulse a fanatical Banzai attack from the southeastern end of the island. This was to be the last organized enemy action, for on the 23d, a final push met only scattered resistance. At approximately midday, Betio was secured.(64)

On the following day, the 2d Marines left the island bound for Hawaii, where a new camp awaited them at Kamuela. However, Camp Tarawa still required three weeks of tedious labor on the part of the Marines of the regiment before they could begin to

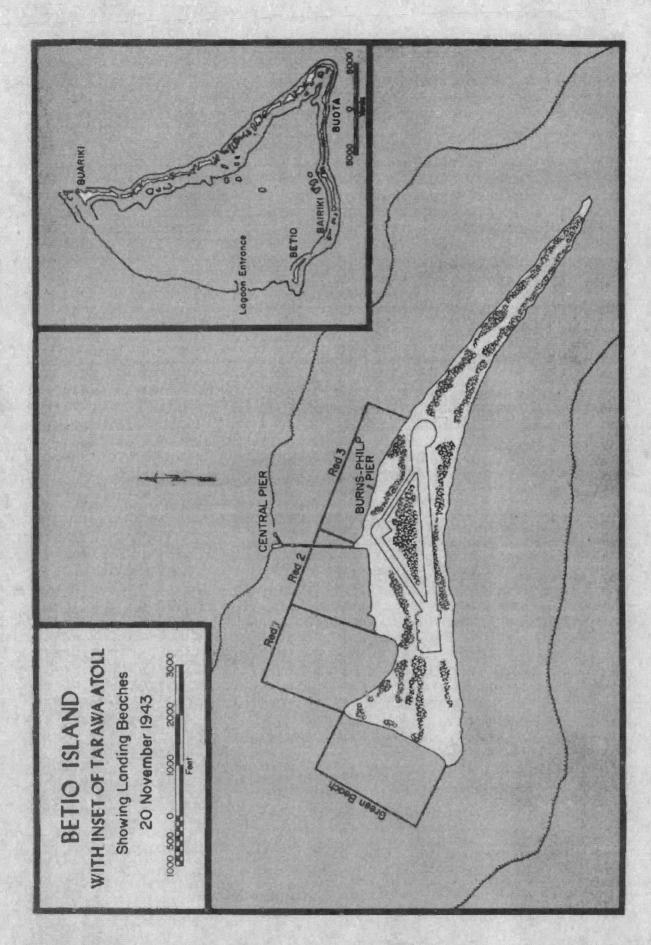

Marine reinforcements wading ashore at Tarawa. (USMC Photo #63516)

Assault on Saipan, 15 Jun 1944. (USMC Photo #89471)

rest and reorganize. Replacements were integrated into the elements of the regiment, and an intensive training program was launched. In the early phases of this program, training emphasis was placed on the lower units, with the newly adopted Marine Corps "fire-team" system being employed by the rifle battalions. The proper functioning of the infantry-tank-artillery-engineer team was stressed in exercises conducted night and day in terrain varying from jungle and cane fields to that more typical of larger volcanic land masses.(65)

The 2d Marines, as part of the 2d Marine Division, culminated its general training by taking part in V Corps amphibious maneuvers held during the latter part of March off the beaches of Maalaea Bay, Maui. The 1st Battalion, 2d Marines, scheduled for a special mission with Company A, Corps Amphibious Reconnaissance Battalion, conducted a special final rehearsal during the period 20-24 May, at Hanalei Bay, Kauai. On 30 May, the 2d Marines, in 2d Marine Division reserve, left Hawaii for further action against the Japanese.

On board ship, Saipan was announced as the target with D-Day set for 15 June. The Marines of the regiment were given detailed information concerning their objective and mission. The 2d Marines was to feint a landing on Tanapag Harbor and then land in support of the actual landing forces near Charan Kanoa.

On 15 June, while elements of the 2d and 4th Marine Divisions made the assault landing in the vicinity of Charan Kanoa, the 2d Marines (less its 1st Battalion) successfully carried out the Tanapag feint in conjunction with the 1st Battalion, 29th Marines, and the 24th Marines. Later in the day, the 3d Battalion and a portion of the 2d Battalion, 2d Marines, landed on the Charan Kanoa beaches to the rear of the assaulting forces. The remainder of the regiment landed on the following day. That night, the 2d Battalion, on line as part of the 6th Marines on the division left, assisted in repelling a violent Japanese tank-infantry counterattack.

On the morning of the 17th, the regiment, as part of the 2d Marine Division, attacked towards Garapan, regulating its advance with that of the 6th Marines to its right.(66) The 2d Marines, the pivot of a corps wheeling movement to the north, marked time for several days just south of Garapan, sending out patrols and waiting for the word to continue the drive northward.

In the afternoon of 23 June, the 2d Battalion (less company F), was detached from the 6th Marines and returned to the 2d Marines as regimental reserve. On the same date, the 2d Battalion, 6th Marines, which had been operating as a part of the 2d Marines, was returned to its parent unit. To replace it, the 1st Battalion, 2d Marines was released by division to the 2d Marines.

By the 24th, the inland drive of the forces had progressed sufficiently to enable the 2d Marines to advance. However, on the outskirts of Garapan the regiment was again held up for several days, patrolling and consolidating its lines, while other elements of the 2d Marine Division slowly pushed through the high ground inland against continuous formidable resistance.

Regimental patrols during this period not only kept the enemy off balance, but also provided an opportunity for the Marines to use various subterfuges to outwit the enemy and gain valuable information. On the 29th, for example, the regiment made a mock attack on a hill occupied by about a platoon of Japanese. After the preparatory fires had been lifted, the 2d Marines opened up with small-arms fire simulating an assault. But, as soon as the Japanese raised up in their positions to repel the assault, artillery, mortars, and heavy machine guns raked the exposed enemy. Several days later, when the regiment actually moved across the position, the litter of Japanese corpses attested to the success of the ruse.

The Regiment's 2d Battalion exchanged positions with the 3d Battalion, 8th Marines on 1 July, with the latter unit assuming a reserve role for the 2d Marines. The regiment drove into Garapan on the following day. The 3d Battalion moved directly into the heart of the city, the largest on Saipan, while the 1st Battalion occupied Sugar Loaf Hill, to the east of Garapan, and tied in with the 6th Marines by nightfall. The 3d Battalion pushed through the rest of the city and onto Mutcho Point on 3 July, with the 1st Battalion reaching the sea north of Garapan that night. The two battalions cleared their sectors on the following day, and then, pinched out by the advance of the 6th Marines, they reverted to Northern Troops and Landing Force Reserve.

The regiment (less its 2d Battalion) was attached to the 4th Marine Division on the morning of 6 July, and advanced with the 23d Marines on its left and the 24th Marines on its right. For the next five days, the 2d Marines, as part of the 4th Marine Division, drove forward against sporadic resistance, finally compressing the enemy into a small area on the northern tip of the island. The 2d now participated in the mop up, and, on the 9th, the island was declared to be secured. Isolated pockets of resistance in the cliffs and wooded areas of the northern part of Saipan kept the Marines of the regiment employed until 23 July.

On the following day, the scene shifted for the 2d Marines as it participated in a feint landing off Tinian town, while the 4th Marine Division landed on the northern tip of the island of Tinian. The 2d Marines also landed over the northern beaches on the 25th, taking positions in the rear of the 8th Marines.(67) The regiment moved up on the right of the 8th Marines on the morning of the 26th, and joined that regiment in a drive toward

Company CP of I/3/2 on Saipan. (USMC Photo #84188)

Assault on Tinian, 21 Jul 1944. (USMC Photo #87230)

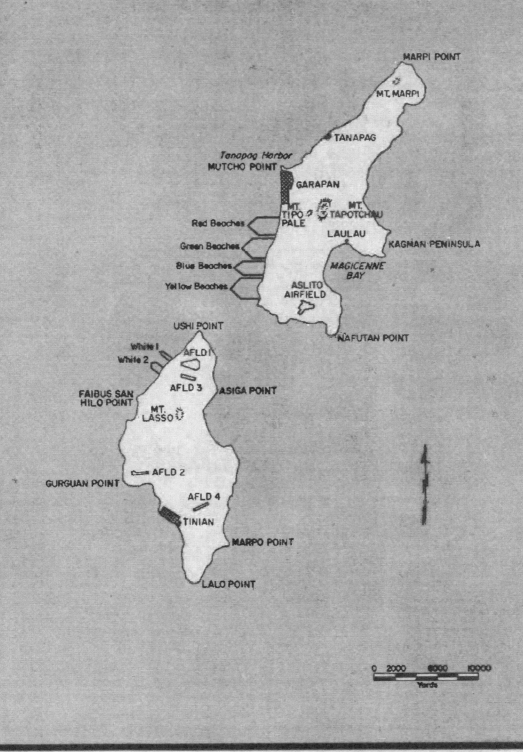

the east coast. Late in the day, the 2d and 8th wheeled to the south, moving rapidly against light resistance.

The 2d Marines reached the cliffs in the Marpo Point area by 31 July and took up blocking positions to prevent the escape of any Japanese to the north. The island of Tinian was declared to be secured on 1 August, and the Marines of the regiment started on the task of mopping up enemy remnants. The 2d's mission was over a week later, when the regiment was returned to Saipan to rest and reorganize.

The 2d Marines remained on Saipan for the next seven months, training under battle conditions as Japanese stragglers continued to harass the occupation forces. On 20 October, the regiment, as part of the 2d Marine Division, passed to the control of III Amphibious Corps for training, planning, and operations. Intensive training continued while high level plans were developed for the next operation.

The 2d Marines sailed for Okinawa on 25 March 1945, as part of the largest amphibious force yet participated in by Marine ground elements. The regiment, with other units of the 2d Marine Division in III Amphibious Corps reserve, was positioned to execute a feint on the Minatoga beaches, on the southeastern tip of the island.(68) The 2d headed for shore, along with other units of the diversionary force; at that moment, the actual landing was being made on the east central shore of Okinawa by other elements of III Amphibious Corps and XXIV Army Corps, comprising the Tenth Army. Not until the landing craft turned about and headed back to the transports and LSTs did the Japanese discover the feint. The 2d did suffer casualties, however, for, as its Marines boarded landing craft for the move to the beaches, a Japanese Kamikaze smashed through the hull of LST 884 killing or wounding a number of the men of Company I 3d Battalion, 2d Marines.(69) The ships bearing the 2d Marines withdrew to deeper water but remained circling in the East China Sea. The threat of further Kamikaze action forced withdrawal of the amphibious force, and the 2d Marine Division (less its 130th Naval Construction Battalion) was returned to Saipan. Here, the Marines of the 2d again commenced an intensive training program. The atomic bombing of Hiroshima and Nagasaki and the entry of Russia into the war against Japan caused a revision of the regiment's plans.

Instead of making an assault on the Japanese homeland, the 2d Marines landed at Nagasaki on 23 September to participate in the occupation of Japan.(70) The regiment was assigned an area consisting of Miyazaki Prefecture and the half of Kagoshima east of Kagoshima Wan, with the mission of checking locations of Japanese military installations and verifying the inventories of Japanese materiel in the assigned area. In addition, the 2d Marines assisted in processing civilian and military personnel, including Formosans, Chinese, and Koreans in addition to the Japanese.

In November 1945, those men of the regiment who had accrued the highest number of points (71) were sent home. In February 1946, the 3d Battalion was returned to the United States and deactivated. Remaining battalions of the 2d Marines were billeted in camps throughout its assigned area and began training in basic subjects, including weapons and combat tactics. The regiment departed Japan for the United States on 13 June, docked at Norfolk on 12 July, and moved overland to Camp Lejeune.(72)

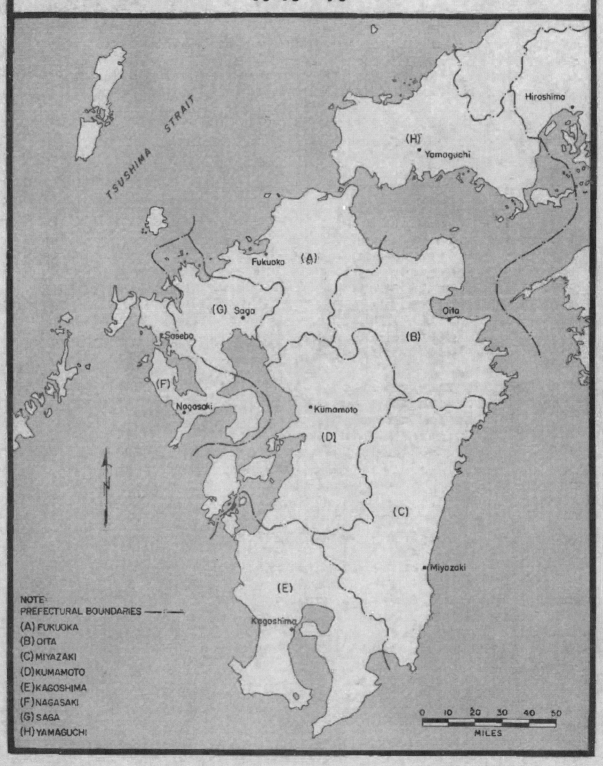

SECTION IV

Decade By Decade

Back "home," the 2d Marines embarked on another intensive training program to prepare for future assignments. As part of the 2d Marine Division, which became the backbone of the newly formed Fleet Marine Force, Atlantic, the 2d Marines was to be employed in vital, varied, and demanding missions over the coming months.

By late 1946, the regiment had an advanced amphibious training program underway. After preparatory work with elements of the Atlantic Fleet, at Little Creek in January and February 1947, the 2d Marines participated in 2d Marine Division landing exercises in the Caribbean in March.(73)

Training continued during the spring and summer months, and on 10 September, the 2d Marines (Rein), or RCT-2, embarked at Morehead City, the port of Camp Lejeune, for six weeks of amphibious exercises at Little Creek. Upon its return from Little Creek on 18 November, the regiment was reduced to battalion strength.(74) Headquarters and Service Company was disbanded; the 1st Battalion was redesignated 2d Marines and reorganized into Companies Headquarters, A, B, and C; and the 2d Battalion was deactivated.

On 5 January 1948, the 2d Marines (Rein) embarked in USS Bexar at Morehead City and sailed for the Mediterranean Sea. It arrived at the island of Malta on 18 January, where its units were transferred to ships of the Sixth Fleet.(75) The Marines of the regiment participated in exercises and maneuvers of the fleet until relieved in March, when the 2d again returned to Camp Lejeune.

The regiment became part of the 1st Provisional Marine Regiment on 1 November, and during the month, it made a two day stopover at Argentia, Newfoundland.(76) The regiment was redesignated 2d Marines (Reinforced), 2d Marine Division on 14 December, and subsequently, took part in fleet maneuvers in the Atlantic and Mediterranean areas.(77) The 2d returned to the United States in April 1949 and on 24 May, again became part of the 1st Provisional Marine Regiment.(78). The 2d Marines returned to a two-battalion strength level on 17 October.

The year 1950 passed in routine fashion for the 2d Marines with the highlight of the year coming in April, when the regiment took part in a division/wing exercise. Training continued for the next year as the regiment made a concerted effort to improve its readiness. War in Korea necessitated the transfer of many of the 2d's personnel to the 1st Marine Division, but the 2d Marines remained oriented towards the Caribbean and the Mediterranean.

The regiment engaged in a major training exercise, LANTFLEX 52 at Vieques from 5 through 13 November 1951. It then returned to Camp Lejeune, where the winter months were spent in preparing for further amphibious training exercises to be held at Little Creek during the latter part of March and early April 1952. On the conclusion of these, the 2d Marines took part in TRAEX I at Vieques. En route back to Lejeune, the regiment was feted by the city of Miami with 9 June being designated "2d Marine Regiment Day." On the 13th, the regiment returned home, "storming" the beaches at Onslow.

BLT 3/2 carried out amphibious exercises at Little Creek in late July prior to serving as the landing force of the Sixth Fleet. During its European tour, the BLT joined NATO forces in exercises at Jutland and cooperated with Greek and Turkish troops in a practice assault landing at Lebedos Bay, Turkey. On 7 February 1953, BLT 3/2 rejoined its parent unit at Camp Lejeune.

The regiment trained in helicopter maneuvers and other assault techniques during the spring in preparation for landings as part of the 2d Marine Division on Vieques from 5 through 28 March. The summer and fall months passed uneventually for the 2d, with BLT 1/2 heading for duty with the Sixth Fleet on 10 September.

In January 1954, the remainder of the regiment engaged in amphibious exercises at Vieques. BLT 1/2/ returned from Europe on 4 February, and, for the summer, the regiment was able to train as a unit. BLT 2/2 embarked for Mediterranean duty on 8 September, and in November, the rest of the regiment took part in LANTFLEX 1-55.

BLT 2/2 returned from its Mediterranean tour on 29 January, so for another summer, the 2d Marines could train as a unit in preparation, this time, for LANTPHIBEX 1-55 to be held at Onslow in October and early November.

The 2d Marines climaxed its 1955 training by participating in TRAEX 1-56 held at Vieques during the first three months of 1956. BLT 3/2 embarked for duty with the Sixth Fleet on 22 August and soon put the previous year's intensive training to good use. During the period 31 October through 3 November, the BLT assisted in the evacuation of United States observers and other nationals from Alexandria, Egypt, and the Gaza Strip, as war threatened between Egypt and Israel.

BLT 3/2 returned to the United States on 1 February 1957, and with all units of the 2d Marines rejoined, it was possible to train as a regimental organization. Training during the early months of the year culminated in a regimental field exer-

Marine infantrymen conducting amphibious training at Onslow Beach. (USMC Photo #A-140402)

Marines assault Onslow Beach during amphibious training exercise, February 1964. (USMC Photo #A19478)

cise held at Lejeune from 1 through 5 April. BLT 1/2 again headed for duty with the Sixth Fleet on 30 April. The 3d Battalion of the regiment took part in TRAMID exercises in June, aiding in the familiarization of Midshipmen in amphibious operations. During the latter part of August and continuing through most of September, the 2d Battalion, 2d Marines furnished the infantry force for BATREX 2-57 held at Vieques.

With the return of BLT 1/2 from southern Europe on 2 October, the 2d Marines increased the intensity of its training as preparations were made tor TRAEX 1-58 to be held at Vieques in February 1958. BLT 2/2 was the next unit of the regiment to head for Mediterranean duty, embarking on 1 May.

This Mediterranean tour was a particularly important one, for the BLT was ashore at Beirut, Lebanon, from 15 July to 15 August, assisting in maintaining order and assuring the preservation of peace. With the tense situation in Lebanon easing, the BLT withdrew in the middle of August, and on 23 October, it was again back at Camp Lejeune, joining the rest of the regiment in further training in the various aspects of amphibious warfare.

From 10 January until 4 June 1959, the 1st Battalion of the regiment provided the infantry force for the 12th Provisional Brigade in BRIGADELEX 59 held in the Caribbean area. Meanwhile, BLT 3/2 departed for the Mediterranean on 26 February, returning on 24 August. In September, the 2d Marines participated in 2d Marine Division exercise TRAEX 3-60 in the Onslow Beach area.

The 60's became a period of intense training for the 2d Marines. It engaged in virtually every type of conditioning related to the accomplishment of the Corps' mission. The primary objective was, of course, to maintain a state of preparedness consistent with Marine Corps doctrine. The 60's witnessed the continued deployment of BLTs to the Mediterranean and the Caribbean, while local exercises from small unit level through that of division/wing size kept the Marines of the 2d ready for any eventuality. With this period came not only training, but events that were to realistically test the results of that preparation. On several occasions the 2d Marines was called upon to respond to world crisis involving American interests.

In the spring months of 1960, the Marines of the 2d, with engineer assistance, improved their instructional facilities at Camp Lejeune by building four classrooms in the regiment's area. As a service to Marine personnel and as an added moral factor, the regiment established the first amateur radio station, W4PKW, at Camp Lejeune. This provided a cross-country radio-telephone system that enabled Marine personnel to call home at no cost.

In the summer months, the 3d Battalion took part in BRIGADELEX 3-60 in the Caribbean area. BLT 2/2 participated in JAMLEX in the Onslow Beach area in the fall as part of continued joint training activities. LANTPHIBEX 1-60, a combination surface and heli-borne assault, was the major exercise of the year, with the 2d Marines (Reinforced) landing over Onslow Beach in a heavy fog. BLT 1/2 made the Mediterranean trip later in the summer, while the Carribbean was the scene of training for others.

On 4 January, 1962, BLT 2/2 conducted a demonstration at Onslow Beach for the Secretary of the Navy. This demonstration involved an amphibious landing with support from the 2d Marine Aircraft Wing at Cherry Point. In February, BLT 3/2 took part in an amphibious landing exercise, MEDLANDEX 1-62, in Sardinia. BLT 3/2 had been conducting training exercises in the Mediterranean since September of 1961.(79)

Foreign dignitaries were often invited to witness Marines in action during training exercises. Such was the case in April, when the 2d Battalion took part in an impressive display of Marine tactics. This operation involved 8,000 Marines from Lejeune and was viewed by representatives from 45 countries. Among the spectators were President John F. Kennedy and the Shah of Iran.(80)

In October and November of 1962, the preparedness of the 2d Marines was tested. President Kennedy ordered a complete naval quarantine against shipment of offensive arms by Russia to Cuba. This action involved more than 40 ships and 20,000 men. The 2d Battalion and other elements of the 2d Marines embarked aboard the USS Chilton and sailed from Morehead City, North Carolina on 16 October for the Cuban area. This crisis eventually subsided but only after bringing the two major world powers to a confrontation that was alarmingly close to the brink of war. The 2d Battalion returned to Camp Lejeune after disembarking at Sunny Point, North Carolina on 3 December.(81)

During the next two years, the 2d Marines engaged in a variety of training exercises. The need for a constant national state of readiness had been clearly shown by the Cuban Missile Crisis.

On 10 July, 1963, BLT 2/2 embarked for a three month training exercise in the Caribbean. While it was engaged in two amphibious landing exercises and conducting counter-insurgency operations over a period of four weeks, the landing team received air support from Provisional Marine Aircraft Group 60. During these operations, the 2d Battalion demonstrated its flexibility. It was forced to reembark twice when hurricanes threatened. In July 1963 when trouble developed in Haiti, the BLT was deployed off the coast of that country for 5 days.

In September of 1963, BLT 3/2 departed for the Mediterranean while BLT 1/2 conducted training exercises in the Caribbean.(82)

The legendary excellence of Marine infantry has been frequently attributed to intensive training at the small unit level. In 1963 a rifle squad from the 3d Battalion won the 2d Marine Division's "Tarawa Award" as the top division squad.(83)

The 2d Marines conducted normal training exercises during 1964. These exercises were punctuated by two large-scale operations. The first such operation, QUICK KICK V, was a mammoth 15-day combined service exercise. On 12 April, elements of the 2d Marines stormed ashore at Onslow Beach with more than 12,000 Marines from the 2d Division. Units from the Army, Navy, and Air Force took part in this exercise which was viewed by the Commandant, General Wallace M. Greene, Jr., and other ranking service leaders, as well as 34 Central and South American journalists.

Late in October, elements of the 2d Marines arrived and disembarked at Huelva, Spain prior to the largest exercise of the year. Taking place at the end of October, STEEL PIKE I involved a joint amphibious landing and assault on the beaches of southern Spain. This landing was made by 28,000 Marines together with Navy and Marine forces of Spain. This operation was of special significance in that it was the largest amphibious assault ever conducted by the Marine Corps in peacetime, as of that date.(84)

The year 1965, as in 1962, witnessed an interruption in the normal training routine for the 2d. Again it was called upon to exhibit its readiness to move out quickly in response to a crisis abroad. During the spring of 1965, the Dominican Republic was beset by internal problems. By late April, the situation had developed into a state of open rebellion endangering U. S. citizens and other foreign nationals. With the mission to protect the people, Marines were called upon to land at Santo Domingo. On 1 May, BLT 1/2, commanded by Lieutenant Colonel J. E. Harrell, was heli-lifted from the Onslow Beach area to the amphibious assault ship, USS Okinawa. Helicopters of Marine Aircraft Group 26 from New River, North Carolina were used to lift the battalion and its equipment. From there, the Okinawa sailed for the Dominican Republic. The BLT remained afloat off the shores of the island republic for one month. The situation cooled off and it returned to Camp Lejeune on 29 May.(85)

With this crisis over, 2d Marines units resumed their normal deployment and training exercises. BLT 2/2 acted as the Marine ready force with the Sixth Fleet in the Mediterranean, while BLT 1/2 departed Camp Lejeune for a three month assignment to the Caribbean. In October BLT 3/2 boarded ships for a five month deployment in the Mediterranean. While deployed, 2d Marines units executed a variety of demanding exercises. During the first two weeks in December, BLT 1/2 took part in PHIBMEMLEX-65. This combined Navy/Marine tactical operation at Vieques,

Puerto Rico involved 3,500 Marines from Camp Lejeune and Cherry Point.(86) Also in December, BLT 3/2 teamed with French Commandos in a vertical assault exercise at Santa Monza, Corsica. Marines utilized helicopters from the French helicopter assault ship Arromanches during the assault. In April of 1966, BLT 2/2 was involved in Special Purpose Exercise-66 (SPECEX-66). More than 1,500 visitors viewed Marine air/ground team tactical readiness. In addition to maintaining training programs throughout the regiment, the 2d acted as host to a variety of reserve units during the month of June.(87)

While the 1st and 3d Marine Divisions were engaged in combat in the Republic of Vietnam, the 2d Marines and other elements of the 2d Marine Division instituted more rigorous and aggressive training programs aimed towards producing a much more combat-oriented Marine. Programs were directed toward guerrilla type tactics. At the same time this changed training technique was being carried on, the 2d Marines were supplying personnel as replacements to the combat-committed units and in time began to receive combat-trained Marines upon completion of their overseas tours. These veterans' knowledge of Vietnam terrain and topography and the experience they had gained helped immeasureably towards enhancing the training of "boot" Marines.

The 1st Battalion departed Camp Lejeune on 2 September for Guantanamo Bay. It relieved 2/2 as part of the ground defense force for the base. Also during September, BLT 3/2 left for the Caribbean where it replaced BLT 3/6 as the Marine Ready force. In December BLT 3/2 was involved in the largest Atlantic Naval and Marine exercises of the year. LANTFLEX-66 took place at Vieques, where more than 42,000 men, 94 ships, and 19 air squadrons participated. Anti-guerrilla tactics were stressed during this exercise and an attempt was made to recreate the type of diverse military problems American forces were currently facing in Southeast Asia.(88)

A new program initiated by the 2d Marines became a significant highlight of its training during 1967. The regiment had the distinction of organizing and training the first scout-sniper platoon in the division. April marked the start of the initial training period which ended with graduation ceremonies on 14 July. This program differed from the usual Marine sniper program in that the students were rigorously trained in intelligence gathering techniques. In addition they received instruction in adjustment of close air and artillery support.(89)

During 1967, the regiment's major training exercise was conducted in March. SHAMROCK, lasting two weeks, featured a regimental-size field exercise held at Camp Pickett, Virginia. (90) In August, BLT 1/2 departed for the Mediterranean where it conducted six major training exercises.

The years 1967 and 1968 found the United States plagued by a variety of domestic problems. Racial strife and civil disturbances were occurring with alarming frequency in the country. Foreseeing the possibility that Marines would be needed to help suppress disturbances, a training program was instituted in June of 1968 to teach the sensitive techniques of riot control. After this new program was fully established, the 2d continued its regular training.

In August of that year (1968) Operation RIVERINE was conducted in the Conhabee and South Edisto river areas of South Carolina. RIVERINE served a dual purpose in that it was designed to develop assault skills of amphibious forces operating in hostile river country, and secondly, to provide an intensive testing period for a new jet-powered armored troop carrier. (91) Also during 1968, BLT 1/2 and 3/2 alternately departed Camp Lejeune for service as the Caribbean ready force of the Sixth Fleet. The 2d Battalion performed training during the latter part of the year at Little Creek, Virginia.

In April 1969, BLT 1/2 participated in a 2d Division amphibious assault exercise SPEX-69 at Onslow Beach. The operation was staged to demonstrate the striking power of the Navy/Marine Air/Ground team.(92) May of 1969 found BLT 2/2 participating in EXOTIC DANCER II, a joint Navy/Marine exercise in the Caribbean area.(93)

The 2d Marines has continually strived to perfect its state of readiness for any eventuality. During its existence of more than half a century, the 2d Marines has performed a variety of military duties throughout much of the world. Whether called upon to fight a battle as bloody as Tarawa, to assist with government rule as in Haiti, or to maintain peace as in Lebanon or the Dominican Republic, the 2d Marines has consistently and effectively executed the mission assigned. The officers and men who are, or who have been, members of the 2d Marines are justly inspired by the record of their regiment--a record that has kept tradition with the past, maintains vigiliant strength for the present, and promises to keep pace with American's needs for the future.

READING LIST

John Miller, Jr., Guadalcanal: The First Offensive---United States Army in World War II---The War in the Pacific. Washington: Historical Division, Department of the Army, 1949. XVIII, 413 pp. illus., maps, notes, bibliog.

    A detailed account of the entire Guadalcanal campaign with emphasis on Army participation. Includes Army staff lists. Contains references to the 2d Marines.

Philip A. Crowl and Edmund G. Love. Seizure of the Gilberts and Marshalls---United States Army in World War II---The War in the Pacific. Washington: Office of the Chief of Military History, Department of the Army, 1955. XVI, 414 pp., illus., maps, bibliog.

    Includes a detailed account of Marine operations on Tarawa and Roi-Namur. Contains references to the 2d Marines.

Philip A. Crowl. Campaign in the Marianas---United States Army in World War II---The War in the Pacific. Washington: Office of the Chief of Military History, Department of the Army, 1960. XIX, 505 pp. illus., maps, bibliog.

    An account of the Army's role in the campaigns on Saipan, Tinian, and Guam. Includes many references to Marines throughout and a succinct analysis of the command relationships between the Army and Marine forces. Contains staff and order of battle lists.

Jane Blakeney. Heroes, U. S. Marine Corps, 1861-1955... Washington: Blakeney, 1957, xviii, 621 pp. illus.

    A general compilation of individual decorations and unit honors, including the texts and citations accompanying the Medal of Honor and unit decorations, and lists of Marines awarded the Navy Cross, Distinguished Service Cross, Distinguished Service Medal, Silver Star, Legion of Merit, Distinguished Flying Cross, Navy and Marine Corps Medal, Soldiers Medal, Life Saving Medal, and Reserve Special Commendation Ribbon.

Commander R. B. Coffey, USN. "A Brief History of the Intervention in Haiti." U. S. Naval Institute Proceedings, v. 48, no. 8 (Aug 1922), pp. 1325-1344.

    An account of the United States' intervention in Haiti, 1915-1934, with emphasis on Marine activities in restoring order and maintaining peace within the country.

Colonel Robert Debs Heinl, Jr., USMC. Soldiers of the Sea; the United States Marine Corps, 1775-1962. Annapolis, Md.: U. S. Naval Institute, 1962. xxxiii, 692 pp. illus., maps, notes, bibliog.

    A general history of the U. S. Marine Corps with emphasis on the 20th Century.

Major Carl W. Hoffman, USMC. Saipan; the Beginning of the End. Washington: Historical Division, Headquarters, U. S. Marine Corps, 1950. vii, 286 pp. illus., maps, notes, bibliog.

    Operations of the V Amphibious Corps, composed of the 2d and 4th Marine Divisions, and the 27th Infantry Division, USA, together with the Army XXIV Corps Artillery on Saipan Island in the Mariana group, 15 Jun - 19 Jul 1944. Includes a Japanese officer's personal account of the last days of Lieutenant General Yoshitsugu Saito, commander of all Japanese forces on Saipan.

Major Carl W. Hoffman, USMC. The Seizure of Tinian. Washington: Historical Division, Headquarters, U. S. Marine Corps, 1951. vi, 169 pp. illus., maps, notes, bibliog.

    Operations of the 2d and 4th Marine Divisions, supported by Army and Marine artillery, on Tinian Island in the Marianas group, 24 Jul - 1 Aug 1944. Includes the text of propaganda leaflets used by American forces on Tinian.

Lieutenant Colonel Frank O. Hough, USMCR, Major Verle E. Ludwig, USMC, and Henry I. Shaw, Jr. Pearl Harbor to Guadalcanal ---History of U. S. Marine Corps Operations in World War II, v. 1. Washington: Historical Branch, G-3 Division, Headquarters, U. S. Marine Corps, 1958. x, 439 pp. illus., maps, notes, bibliog.

    Operations of Marine Corps units in Samoa, from 21 Dec 1945; Iceland, 7 Jul 1941 - 8 Mar 1942; Wake Island, 19 Aug - 23 Dec 1941; Philippines, Jul 1941 - 6 May 1942; Guam, 8-10 Dec 1941; the Battle of Midway, 4-5 Jun 1942; Guadalcanal, 7 Aug 1942 - 9 Feb 1943. Contains in introductory section on the pre-war development of amphibious techniques and doctrine (pp. 1-56). Appendices include the task organization of Marine units in the Wake, Philippines, Midway, and Guadalcanal operations, a table of casualties, and unit commendations awarded for the period.

Jeter A. Isley and Philip A. Crowl. The U. S. Marines and Amphibious War: Its Theory and Its Practice in the Pacific. Princeton, N. J.: Princeton University Press, 1951. x, 636 pp. maps, notes.

    An interpretive history of the development of amphibious weapons, tactics, and doctrine by the Marine Corps during World War II. Includes an introductory section covering the pre-war evolution of amphibious warfare and contains a chapter devoted to the Tentative Landing Operations Manual which formed the basis for all subsequent amphibious doctrine.

Richard W. Johnston. Follow Me; the Story of the Second Marine Division in World War II. New York: Random House, 1948. xi, 305 pp. illus., maps.

    An account of the division's campaigns: Tulagi, Gavutu, 7-10 Aug 1942; Guadalcanal, 14 Sep 1942 - 19 Feb 1943; Tarawa, 20 Nov - 4 Dec 1943; Saipan, 15 Jun - 9 Jul 1944; Tinian, 24 Jul - 3 Aug 1944; Okinawa, 1 Apr - 15 Jul 1945. Includes a table of casualties, photographs of Medal of Honor recipients and commanding officers, and the text of the Presidential Unit Citation awarded for the assault and capture of Tarawa.

Captain Edmund G. Love, USA. The 27th Infantry Division in World War II. Washington: Infantry Journal Press, 1949. viii, 677 pp. illus., maps.

    A narrative of the Army division which served with the V Amphibious Corps in the Gilberts and on Saipan, and with the Tenth Army in the assault on Okinawa. Many references to Marines throughout.

Captain Herbert L. Merillat, USMCR. The Island; a History of the First Marine Division on Guadalcanal, August 7 - December 9, 1942. Boston: Houghton-Mifflin, 1944. xvi, 283 pp. illus., ports, maps.

    A colorful account of the campaign by a combat correspondent. Contains references to the 2d Marines.

Lieutenant Colonel Clyde H. Metcalf, USMC. "The Marines in China." Marine Corps Gazette, v. 22, no. 3 (Sep 1938), pp. 35-37, 53-58.

    A narrative of Marine activities in China 1900-1901, 1911-1912, and other years, including some discussion of tactics employed against bandits and guerrillas.

Bernard C. Nalty. The United States Marines in the Gilberts Campaign---Marine Corps Historical Reference Series, No. 28. Washington: Historical Branch, G-3 Division, Headquarters, U. S. Marine Corps, 1961. 9pp. bibliog.

    A brief account of the capture of Tarawa.

Captain James B. Stockman, USMC. The Battle for Tarawa. Washington: Historical Section, Division of Public Information, Headquarters, U. S. Marine Corps, 1947. vii, 86 pp. illus., maps, notes, bibliog.

    Operations of the 2d Marine Division while serving under the V Amphibious Corps on Tarawa Atoll, principally Betio Island, and brief accounts of the seizures of Apamama, Abaiang, Marakei, and Mainana Atolls in the Gilberts, 20 Nov - 4 Dec 1943.

Benis M. Frank and Henry I. Shaw, Jr. Victory and Occupation---History of U. S. Marine Corps Operations in World War II, v. V, Washington: Historical Branch, G-3 Division, Headquarters, U. S. Marine Corps, 1968. xiii, 945 pp. illus., maps, notes, bibliog.

    A narrative covering Marine Corps activities in the Okinawa invasion and the occupation of Japan and North China as well as the little known story of Marine Prisoners of War.

APPENDIX A

Notes

(1) *Muster Rolls*, 2d Regiment, Jan01 (Reference Branch, Historical Division, HQMC). hereafter *Muster Rolls* with unit, month, and year.

(2) "Report of the Commandant of the Marine Corps" in *Report of the Secretary of the Navy*, 1901, p. 1228, hereafter *CMC Report* with year; "History of U. S. Marine Corps Activities at Subic Bay, P. I., 1899-1955," MS, (HistBr, G-3 Archives, HQMC, Jun56), p. 11, hereafter *Subic Bay*.

(3) *Subic Bay*, p. 34.

(4) Joel D. Thacker, "Stand Gentlemen, He Served on Samar!" MS, (HistBr, G-3 Archives, HQMC, Mar45).

(5) *Subic Bay*, p. 23.

(6) The need for such a base was pointed out by Navy experience in the Spanish-American War. Special Report of the Commander in Chief, U. S. Asiatic Fleet, Appendix Q to "Report of Chief of the Bureau Navigation," *Report of the Secretary of the Navy*, 1903, p. 651.

(7) *Subic Bay*, p. 25.

(8) *CMC Report*, 1912, p. 590.

(9) *Muster Rolls*, Companies B, C, and E, 2d Regiment, Dec11; Company A, 2d Regiment, Aug12.

(10) *Muster Rolls*, 2d Regiment, Jan14; *Subic Bay*, p. 35.

(11) *Muster Rolls*, 2d Regiment, 1st Provisional Brigade, Dec03. In the early years of 1900, several instances occurred when more than one regiment with the same designation existed concurrently because of the forming of provisional regiments to handle specific missions. Each regiment designated "Second" or "2d" in muster rolls and unit diaries is chronologically treated herein as of its date of activation.

(12) Clyde H. Metcalf, *A History of the United States Marine Corps* (New York: G. P. Putnam's Sons, 1939), p. 294ff, hereafter Metcalf, *USMC History*.

(13) *CMC Report*, 1904, p. 1192.

(14) *Muster Rolls*, 2d Regiment, 1st Provisional Brigade, Feb04.

(15) United States intervention in Cuba was authorized by the Platt Amendment which implemented certain provisions of the Treaty of Paris. Thomas A. Baily, *A Diplomatic History of the American People* (New York: F. S. Crofts & Co., 1947), p. 549, hereafter Bailey, *Diplomatic History*.

(16) *Muster Rolls*, 4th Expeditionary Battalion, Sep06.

(17) *Muster Rolls*, 2d Regiment, 1st Expeditionary Brigade, Oct06.

(18) *Muster Rolls*, 2d Expeditionary Regiment, Dec09.

(19) *CMC Report*, 1910, p. 803.

(20) *Muster Rolls*, 2d Regiment, 1st Provisional Brigade, Mar11. p. 457.

(21) *Muster Rolls*, 2d Regiment, 1st Provisional Brigade, Jun11.

(22) *Muster Rolls*, 2d Provisional Regiment, May12.

(23) *Muster Rolls*, 2d Provisional Regiment, Aug12; *War Diary*, 1st Provisional Brigade, Marines, May-Aug12, (Cuba File, HistBr, G-3 Archives, HQMC).

(24) Bailey, *Diplomatic History*, p. 559.

(25) *Muster Rolls*, 2d Provisional Regiment, Sep12.

(26) *CMC Report*, 1904, p. 1193; Metcalf, *USMC History*, p. 340.

(27) *Muster Rolls*, 2d Regiment, 2d Provisional Brigade.

(28) *Muster Rolls*, 2d Regiment, Expeditionary Force, USMC, May13.

(29) *Muster Rolls*, 2d Regiment, Expeditionary Force, USMC, Jun13; Metcalf, *USMC History*, p. 298.

(30) *CMC Report*, 1913, p. 543; *Muster Rolls*, 1st Advance Base Regiment, Jun13. This regiment was designed to be made up of specialists for fixed defense activities of a permanent advance base force. The 2d Advance Base Regiment was to be composed of infantry and artillery for mobile defense service by the force.

(31) *CMC Report*, 1914, p. 470ff. With the formation of this brigade the Advance Base Force came into being. It was composed of two permanently organized regiments, each tailored to its specific part in the advance base force concept. At the same time, numerical designations for companies were adopted to alleviate the problem of having more than one company A, for example, in any one expeditionary force.

(32) <u>Muster Rolls</u>, 1st Regiment, Feb14.

(33) Kenneth W. Condit and Edwin T. Turnbladh, <u>Hold High the Torch</u>, <u>A History of the 4th Marines</u> (Washington: HistBr, G-3, HQMC, 1960), p. 12.

(34) <u>CMC Report</u>, 1914, p. 470ff.

(35) <u>CMC Report</u>, <u>1915</u>, p. 662.

(36) <u>Muster Rolls</u>, 1st Regiment, Dec14.

(37) D. A. Greber, <u>Crisis Diplomacy</u> (Washington: Public Affairs Press, 1959), p. 155.

(38) <u>CMC Report</u>, <u>1915</u>, p. 662.

(39) <u>Muster Rolls</u>, 2d Regiment, May-Jul16.

(40) James H. McCrocklin, <u>Garde d' Haiti; Twenty Years of Organization and Training by the United States Marine Corps</u> (Annapolis: U. S. Naval Institute, 1956).

(41) <u>Muster Rolls</u>, 10th Company, 2d Regiment, Nov16.

(42) <u>Muster Rolls</u>, 2d Regiment and enumerated companies, Dec19.

(43) <u>Muster Rolls</u>, 2d Regiment, Jan20.

(44) Metcalf, <u>USMC History</u>, p. 395ff.

(45) <u>CMC Report</u>, <u>1923</u>, p. 969.

(46) <u>Muster Rolls</u>, enumerated companies, 2d Regiment, Jul24.

(47) <u>Muster Rolls</u>, Headquarters Company, 2d Regiment, Jun25.

(48) <u>Muster Rolls</u>, 2d Regiment and enumerated companies, Jul25.

(49) <u>Muster Rolls</u>, 63d and 54th Companies, 2d Regiment, Mar26.

(50) <u>Muster Rolls</u>, 2d Marines, Jan33.

(51) <u>Muster Rolls</u>, 2d Marines, Jul-Aug34.

(52) <u>Muster Rolls</u>, 2d Marines, Feb41.

(53) Richard W. Johnston, <u>Follow Me! The Story of the Second Marine Division in World War II</u> (New York: Random House, 1949), p. 13ff, hereafter Johnston, <u>2d MarDiv History</u>.

(54) Division Training Order #21-42, dated 28 May 42; Units were 2d Marines; 2d Bn, 10th Marines; Co C, 2d Tank Bn; 1st Plat, Btry A (AA) SW/Bn; 1st Plat, Btry B (AT) SW/Bn; Co A, 2d EngBn; Co A, 2d Pion Bn plus CommTm #1; Co C, 2d SerBn; Co A, 2d AmphTrBn, plus Repair Sec H&S Co, 2d SerBn; Det PX, 2d SerBn; Det Commissary Unit, 2d SerBn; Two Bakery Units, Bakery Section, Commissary Platoon.

(55) Isely and Crowl, USMC Amphibious War, (Princeton, New Jersey: Princeton University Press, 1951), p. 114; John L. Zimmerman, The Guadalcanal Campaign (Washington: HistBr, G-3, HQMC, 1949), p. 22, hereafter Zimmerman, Guadalcanal.

(56) LtCol Frank O. Hough, Maj Verle E. Ludwig, and Henry I. Shaw, Jr., Pearl Harbor to Guadalcanal, History of U. S. Marine Corps Operations in World War II, Vol. I (Washington: HistBr, G-3, HQMC, 1958), p. 263, and, unless otherwise cited, the source of the following account of the 2d Marines in the Guadalcanal area.

(57) Zimmerman, Guadalcanal, Map following p. 94.

(58) Zimmerman, Guadalcanal, p. 112.

(59) The 2d was stationed at Camp McKay's Crossing, where all attached units reverted to their parent control on 7 February. Muster Rolls, 2d Marine Division, Feb43.

(60) Capt James R. Stockman, The Battle for Tarawa (Washington: Historical Section, Division of Public Information, HQMC, 1947), p. 3, and, unless otherwise cited, the source of the following account of the 2d Marines on Tarawa.

(61) Johnston, 2dMarDiv History, p. 98ff.

(62) Muster Rolls, 2d Marine Division, Nov43.

(63) Johnston, 2dMarDiv History, p. 132.

(64) For His leadership, tactics, and devotion to duty, Colonel Shoup received the Nation's highest award, the Congressional Medal of Honor.

(65) Maj Carl W. Hoffman, Saipan: The Beginning of the End (Washington: Historical Division, HQMC, 1950), pp. 30-31, and, unless otherwise cited, the source of the following account of the 2d Marines on Saipan.

(66) At this time, the regiment was composed of its own 3d Battalion and the 2d Battalion, 6th Marines. Its 2d Battalion was still attached to the 6th Marines, while its 1st Battalion was under 2d Marine Division control. One company of the 1st Battalion, 2d Marines returned to 2d Marine control late in the afternoon of the 17th.

(67) Maj Carl W. Hoffman, *The Seizure of Tinian* (Washington: Historical Division, HQMC, 1951), p. 69, and, unless otherwise cited, the source of the following account of the 2d Marines in Tinian.

(68) Maj Charles S. Nichols and Henry I. Shaw, Jr., *Okinawa: Victory in the Pacific* (Washington: HistBr, G-3, HQMC, 1955), p. 63, and, unless otherwise cited, the source of the following account of the 2d Marines at Okinawa.

(69) Johnston, *2dMarDiv History*, p. 262. The word Kamikaze which is Japanese for divine wind was the name of those manned aircraft deliberately crashed on the enemy in a suicidal attempt to forestall defeat.

(70) Henry I. Shaw, Jr., "The United States Marines in the Occupation of Japan," MS (HistBr, G-3, HQMC, 1960), p. 32, and, unless otherwise cited, the source of the following account of the 2d Marines in Japan.

(71) Points were awarded for time overseas, combat operations, participated in, personal citations, and dependents.

(72) *Muster Rolls*, 2d MarDiv, Jun-Jul46.

(73) *The Camp Lejeune Globe* (Camp Lejeune, North Carolina, 18Dec46 - 26Mar47) and, unless otherwise cited, the source of the remainder of the 2d Marines' narrative.

(74) This reduction was part of a 2d Marine Division reorganization as announced by Division General Order #157-47, dated, 8Nov47; *Muster Rolls*, 2dMarDiv, nov47.

(75) The 2d Marines was redesignated 2d Marines (Reinforced) in compliance with CG, FMFLant confidential dispatch 24135, dated Dec47; *Muster Rolls*, 2d MarDiv, Jan48. Mediterranean duty for the regiment, BLTs thereof, and other Marine units during the years to the present (1960) involved participating as the landing force of the Sixth Fleet patrolling the Mediterranean and North Atlantic waters in accordance with United States policy of promoting peace and stability in the area.

(76) *Muster Rolls*, 1stProvMarReg, Nov48.

(77) CO, Hq., 1stProvMarReg, confidential letter, Serial 02, dated 13Dec48: *Muster Rolls*, 2dMarDiv, Dec48.

(78) CG, 2dMarDiv letter, Serial 9926, dated 31May49: *Muster Rolls*, 1stProvMarReg, May49.

(79) The Camp Lejeune Globe (Camp Lejeune, North Carolina) 16Feb462.

(80) Globe, 19Apr62.

(81) Unit Diary, Headquarters Company, 2d Regiment, 1962.

(82) Ibid., 14Nov63.

(83) Ibid., 30Jan64.

(84) Unit Diary, Headquarters Company, 2d Regiment, 1964.

(85) The Camp Lejeune Globe, 3Jun65.

(86) Ibid., 2Dec65.

(87) Ibid., 2Jun66.

(88) Ibid., 22Dec66.

(89) Command Chronology, 2d Marines, July 1966 - December 1967, (enc. 5).

(90) Post Exercise Report 2d Marines, 1967 (Exercise "Shamrock").

(91) Globe, 23Aug68.

(92) Ibid., 25Apr69.

(93) Ibid., 18May69.

APPENDIX B

Commanding Officers, 2d Marines, 1901-1960

Introduction

Since 1901, there have been a number of regimental organizations in the Marine Corps bearing the designation "Second." The following list enumerates the Commanding Officers of all of these regiments. In the early days, there were instances in which there were more than one "2d Regiment" at the same time. Each of these has been entered in the list chronologically by the date of activation. A series of asterisks have been used at the end of particular rosters to indicate total disbandment of a regiment. Absence of asterisks between regimental headings indicates a redesignation. Single asterisks indicate those Commanding Officers later to become Commandants of the Marine Corps.

2d Regiment, 1st Brigade

Note: Organized in the Philippines upon the forming of the provisional 1st Brigade in January 1901.

Rank	Name	Dates
LtCol	Allen C. Kelton	1 Jan 1901 - 29 Sep 1901
Maj	Randolph Dickens	30 Sep 1901 - 17 Oct 1901
LtCol	Otway C. Berryman	18 Oct 1901 - 19 Jan 1903
Maj	Randolph Dickens	20 Jan 1903 - 4 Feb 1903
Maj	Lincoln Karmany	5 Feb 1903 - 7 Aug 1903
Capt	Arthur J. Matthews	8 Aug 1903 - 14 Aug 1903
Capt	Eli K. Cole	15 Aug 1903 - 28 Aug 1903
Maj	Lincoln Karmany	29 Aug 1903 - 15 Apr 1904
Maj	Charles A. Doyen	16 Apr 1904 - 24 Jan 1905
Capt	Philip D. Brown	25 Jan 1905 - 28 Feb 1905
Maj	Charles A. Doyen	1 Mar 1905 - 7 Apr 1905
Maj	Joseph H. Pendleton	8 Apr 1905 - 5 Jul 1905
Maj	Lewis C. Lucas	6 Jul 1905 - 7 Sep 1905
Maj	Eli K. Cole	8 Sep 1905 - 16 Sep 1906
Capt	Smedley D. Butler	17 Sep 1906 - 20 Nov 1906
Maj	Eli K. Cole	21 Nov 1906 - 28 Aug 1907
Capt	John W. Wright	29 Aug 1907 - 3 Sep 1907
Maj	Eli K. Cole	4 Sep 1907 - 23 Nov 1907
Capt	Hiram I. Bearss	24 Nov 1907 - 29 Feb 1908
Capt	John W. Wright	1 Mar 1908 - 9 Nov 1908
Capt	William H. Clifford	10 Nov 1908 - 3 Dec 1908
Maj	William N. McKelvy	4 Dec 1908 - 10 Nov 1909
Maj	Thomas C. Treadwell	11 Nov 1909 - 24 Jan 1910
LtCol	Joseph H. Pendleton	25 Jan 1910 - 13 Jan 1911
Capt	Alexander S. Williams	14 Jan 1911 - 15 Feb 1911

LtCol	Joseph H. Pendleton	16 Feb 1911 - 7 Jul 1911
Capt	Herbert J. Hirshinger	8 Jul 1911 - 7 Aug 1911
LtCol	Joseph H. Pendleton	8 Aug 1911 - 11 Sep 1911
Capt	John W. Wadleigh	12 Sep 1911 - 16 Sep 1911
Capt	James McE. Huey	17 Sep 1911 - 9 Oct 1911
LtCol	Joseph H. Pendleton	10 Oct 1911 - 11 Oct 1911
Capt	James McE. Huey	12 Oct 1911 - 17 Oct 1911
LtCol	Joseph H. Pendleton	18 Oct 1911 - 22 Nov 1911
Capt	James McE. Huey	23 Nov 1911 - 25 Nov 1911
LtCol	Joseph H. Pendleton	26 Nov 1911 - 19 Dec 1911
Capt	James McE. Huey	20 Dec 1911 - 22 Dec 1911
LtCol	Joseph H. Pendleton	23 Dec 1911 - 17 Jan 1912
Capt	James McE. Huey	18 Jan 1912 - 31 Jan 1912
Col	Joseph H. Pendleton	1 Feb 1912 - 6 May 1912
LtCol	Laurence H. Moses	7 May 1912 - 15 Nov 1912
Capt	Herbert J. Hirshinger	16 Nov 1912 - 1 Dec 1912
LtCol	Laurence H. Moses	2 Dec 1912 - 23 Mar 1913
Capt	Benjamin F. Rittenhouse	24 Mar 1913 - 28 Apr 1913
LtCol	Laurence H. Moses	29 Apr 1913 - 20 Jan 1914

* * * * *

2d Regiment, 1st Provisional Brigade

Note: Organized at Philadelphia for duty in Panama.

LtCol	Littleton W. T. Waller	26 Dec 1903 - 20 Feb 1904

* * * * *

2d Regiment, 1st Expeditionary Brigade

Note: Organized at Camp Columbia, Guantanamo Bay, Cuba, by redesignation of 4th Expeditionary Battalion.

LtCol	Franklin J. Moses	8 Oct 1906 - 31 Oct 1906

* * * * *

2d Regiment, Expeditionary Brigade

Note: Organized at Philadelphia for duty in Panama.

LtCol	Eli K. Cole	12 Dec 1909 - 25 Apr 1910

* * * * *

2d Regiment, 1st Provisional Brigade

Note: Organized at Philadelphia for duty in Cuba.

Col	Franklin J. Moses	11 Mar 1911 - 14 Jun 1911

* * * * *

2d Provisional Regiment

Note: Organized at Philadelphia for duty in Cuba.

Col	James E. Mahoney	27 May 1912 - 13 Jul 1912
Capt	Philip S. Brown	14 Jul 1912 - 1 Aug 1912

* * * * *

2d Provisional Regiment

Note: Organized at Philadelphia for duty in the Dominican Republic.

Col	Franklin J. Moses	27 Sep 1912 - 7 Dec 1912

* * * * *

2d Regiment, 2d Provisional Brigade

Note: Organized at Philadelphia for duty in Cuba.

Col	Joseph H. Pendleton	19 Feb 1913 - 30 Apr 1913

2d Regiment, Expeditionary Force, USMC

Col	Joseph H. Pendleton	1 May 1913 - 1 Jun 1913

* * * * *

1st Advance Base Regiment

Note: This unit was organized at Advance Base School, Marine Barracks, Philadelphia.

LtCol	Charles G. Long	19 Jun 1913 - 17 Feb 1914

1st Regiment, 1st Advance Base Brigade

LtCol	Charles G. Long	18 Feb 1914 - 21 Apr 1914

1st Regiment, 1st Brigade

LtCol	Charles G. Long	22 Apr 1914 - 5 May 1914
Col	James E. Mahoney	6 May 1914 - 4 Dec 1914
LtCol	Charles G. Long	5 Dec 1914 - 7 Aug 1915
Col	Theodore P. Kane	8 Aug 1915 - 15 Aug 1915
Col	Eli K. Cole	16 Aug 1915 - 8 May 1916
LtCol	Laurence H. Moses	9 May 1916 - 24 Jun 1916
Col	Eli K. Cole	25 Jun 1916 - 30 Jun 1916

Note: 1st and 2d Regiments exchanged designations in Santo Domingo, Dominican Republic, 1 Jul 1916.

Col	Eli K. Cole	1 Jul 1916 - 30 Nov 1916
LtCol	Philip M. Bannon	1 Dec 1916 - 10 Jan 1918
Maj	Richard S. Hooker	11 Jan 1918 - 31 Mar 1918
Maj	John W. Wadleigh	1 Apr 1918 - 28 Apr 1918
LtCol	Richard S. Hooker	29 Apr 1918 - 14 Nov 1918
LtCol	Thomas H. Brown	15 Nov 1918 - 28 Nov 1918
LtCol	Richard S. Hooker	29 Nov 1918 - 9 Dec 1918
Maj	Henry S. Green	10 Dec 1918 - 17 Jan 1919
LtCol	Richard S. Hooker	18 Jan 1919 - 20 Jul 1919
LtCol	Thomas H. Brown	21 Jul 1919 - 10 Sep 1919
Maj	Charles A. Lutz	11 Sep 1919 - 2 Oct 1919
Col	Randolph C. Berkeley	3 Oct 1919 - 20 Oct 1921
Col	George Van Orden	21 Oct 1921 - 8 Apr 1923
LtCol	William H. Pritchett	9 Apr 1923 - 9 Jul 1923
Col	William N. McKelvy	10 Jul 1923 - 10 Nov 1924
Maj	Maurice E. Shearer	11 Nov 1924 - 9 Jan 1925
Col	William N. McKelvy	10 Jan 1925 - 10 Jun 1925
Maj	Maurice E. Shearer	11 Jun 1925 - 30 Jun 1925
Col	Harold C. Snyder	1 Jul 1925 - 8 Apr 1926
Col	Macker Bab	9 Apr 1926 - 30 Jun 1927
Maj	Archibald Young	1 Jul 1927 - 19 Aug 1927
Col	Presley M. Rixey, II	20 Aug 1927 - 21 May 1929
Col	Richard P. Williams	22 May 1929 - 30 May 1930
Col	Edward B. Manwaring	31 May 1930 - 15 May 1932
Col	Henry G. Bartlett	16 May 1932 - 16 Jun 1932
Col	James T. Buttrick	17 Jun 1932 - 31 Dec 1932

2d Marines

Note: Redesignated by authority Article 5-41(4), Marine Corps Manual.

Col	James T. Buttrick	1 Jan 1933 - 27 Dec 1933
Col	Eli T. Fryer	28 Dec 1933 - 31 May 1934
Maj	Samuel P. Budd	1 Jun 1934 - 15 Aug 1934

Note: On 15 Aug 1934, the 2d Marines disbanded upon the evacuation of the 1st Brigade from the Republic of Haiti.

* * * * *

2d Marines

Note: Reactivated at Marine Corps Base, San Diego, as an integral part of the 2d Marine Division.

Col	Joseph C. Fegan	1 Feb 1941 - 24 Oct 1941
LtCol	Roy C. Swink	25 Oct 1941 - 20 Nov 1941
Col	John M. Arthur	21 Nov 1941 - 6 Jun 1943
Col	William M. Marshall	7 Jun 1943 - 18 Jul 1943
LtCol	Arnold F. Johnston	19 Jul 1943 - 26 Sep 1943
Col	William M. Marshall	27 Sep 1943 - 7 Nov 1943
*Col	David M. Shoup	8 Nov 1943 - 23 Dec 1943

LtCol	Lloyd Russell	24 Dec 1943 - 1 Jan 1944
LtCol	Walter J. Stuart	2 Jan 1944 - 3 Sep 1944
Col	Richard M. Cutts, Jr.	4 Sep 1944 - 24 Oct 1945
LtCol	Clarence J. O'Donnell	25 Oct 1945 - 17 Apr 1946
LtCol	Ronald B. Wilde	18 Apr 1946 - 1 Aug 1946
Col	Francis H. Brink	2 Aug 1946 - 18 Nov 1947

2d Marines

Note: As of 18 Nov 1947, the 2d Marines was reduced to battalion strength with the 1st Battalion, 2d Marines, being designated as "2d Marines."

Col	Francis H. Brink	19 Nov 1947 - 6 Apr 1948
LtCol	Max C. Chapman	7 Apr 1948 - 30 Apr 1948
LtCol	Wilbur F. Meyerhoff	1 May 1948 - 18 May 1948
Col	Randall M. Victory	19 May 1948 - 31 Oct 1948

2d Marines, 1st Provisional Marine Regiment

Col	Randall M. Victory	1 Nov 1948 - 21 Nov 1948
LtCol	Harold Granger	22 Nov 1948 - 13 Dec 1948

2d Marines, Reinforced, 2d Marine Division

LtCol	Harold Granger	14 Dec 1948 - 23 May 1949

2d Marines, 1st Provisional Marine Regiment

LtCol	Harold Granger	24 May 1949 - 31 Jul 1949
LtCol	Jack W. Hawkins	1 Aug 1949 - 2 Oct 1949
Col	Randall M. Victory	3 Oct 1949 - 16 Oct 1949

2d Marines

Note: On 17 Oct 1949, the 2d Marines was reorganized and enlarged to full regimental status.

Col	Randall M. Victory	17 Oct 1949 - 1 Feb 1950
LtCol	Gould P. Groves	2 Feb 1950 - 25 Feb 1950
Col	Reynolds H. Hayden	26 Feb 1950 - 28 Apr 1950
LtCol	Gould P. Groves	29 Apr 1950 - 4 Aug 1950
	None Designated	5 Aug 1950 - 10 Aug 1950
LtCol	Walter F. Layer	11 Aug 1950 - 5 Sep 1950
Col	Reynolds H. Hayden	6 Sep 1950 - 20 Jul 1951
Col	Bruno Hochmuth	21 Jul 1951 - 29 Jul 1952
Col	Robert F. Scott	30 Jul 1952 - 16 Aug 1953
LtCol	William A. Stiles	17 Aug 1953 - 19 Oct 1953
Col	David W. Stonecliffe	20 Oct 1953 - 9 Jul 1954

Col	George W. Hayes	10 Jul 1954 - 24 Aug 1955
Col	William R. Collins	25 Aug 1955 - 5 Jul 1956
Col	Robert E. Cushman, Jr.	6 Jul 1956 - 19 Feb 1957
Col	Raymond L. Dean	20 Feb 1957 - 15 Jul 1957
LtCol	Tillman N. Peters	16 Jul 1957 - 1 Aug 1957
Col	John J. Gormley	2 Aug 1957 - 25 Jun 1958
Col	Charles R. Baker	26 Jun 1958 - 1 Dec 1959
Col	Erma A. Wright	2 Dec 1959 - 12 Jun 1960
Col	Charles W. Kelly, Jr.	13 Jun 1960 - 16 Jun 1961
Col	Alfred L. Booth	17 Jun 1961 - 4 Apr 1962
Col	Robert M. Richards	5 Apr 1962 - 2 Jul 1963
LtCol	John B. Bristow	3 Jul 1963 - 31 Jul 1963
Col	James Taul	1 Aug 1963 - 1 Aug 1964
Col	Paul M. Smith	2 Aug 1964 - 6 Feb 1965
Col	Charles H. Brush, Jr.	7 Feb 1965 - 7 Jun 1966
Col	William R. Burgoyne, Jr.	8 Jun 1966 - 31 Aug 1967
Col	Leroy V. Corbett	1 Sep 1967 - 18 Feb 1968
Col	William E. Barber	19 Feb 1968 - 13 May 1969
Col	Lawrence J. Bradley	14 May 1969 - 28 May 1970
LtCol	David M. Twomey	29 May 1970 -

APPENDIX C

Chronology - Provisional Regiments

1 Jan 1901	2d Regiment organized at Cavite, Philippine Islands.
20 Jan 1914	2d Regiment dissolved by reassignment of elements.
26 Dec 1903	2d Regiment, 1st Provisional Brigade organized at League Island, Pennsylvania, for duty in Panama.
14 Feb 1904	2d Regiment, 1st Provisional Brigade disbanded at Panama.
8 Oct 1906	2d Regiment, 1st Expeditionary Brigade formed in Cuba.
31 Oct 1906	2d Regiment, 1st Expeditionary Brigade disbanded in Cuba.
12 Dec 1909	2d Expeditionary Regiment formed at Philadelphia.
25 Apr 1910	2d Expeditionary Regiment disbanded at Philadelphia.
9 Mar 1911	2d Regiment, 1st Provisional Brigade formed at Philadelphia.
14 Jun 1911	2d Regiment, 1st Provisional Brigade disbanded at Philadelphia.
27 May 1912	2d Provisional Regiment formed at Philadelphia for duty in Cuba.
1 Aug 1912	2d Provisional Regiment dissolved in Cuba.
27 Sep 1912	2d Provisional Regiment formed at Philadelphia for duty in Santo Domingo.
7 Dec 1912	2d Provisional Regiment returned to and disbanded at Philadelphia.
19 Feb 1913	2d Regiment, 2d Provisional Brigade formed at Philadelphia intended for duty in Mexico but went to Cuba awaiting an emergency.
1 May 1913	Redesignated 2d Regiment, Expeditionary Force.
1 Jun 1913	2d Regiment, Expeditionary Force returned to and disbanded at Philadelphia.

APPENDIX D

Chronology, 2d Marines

19 Jun 1913	1st Advance Base Regiment organized at Philadelphia.
23 Dec 1913	Redesignated as 1st Advance Base Regiment, Advance Base Brigade.
18 Feb 1914	Redesignated as 1st Regiment, Advance Base Brigade.
22 Apr 1914	1st Regiment landed at Vera Cruz, Mexico.
23 Nov 1914	1st Regiment departed Mexico for Philadelphia.
15 Aug 1915	1st Regiment relocated to Cape Haitien.
1 Jul 1916	1st Regiment redesignated 2d Regiment.
1 Jan 1933	2d Regiment redesignated as 2d Marines.
15 Aug 1934	2d Marines deactivated in Haiti.
1 Feb 1941	2d Marines reactivated at Marine Corps Base, San Diego.
1 Jul 1942	2d Marines deployed to Koro Island.
7 Aug 1942 to 31 Jan 1943	2d Marines participated in Solomon Islands campaign.
6 Feb 1943	2d Marines redeployed to Wellington, New Zealand.
20-24 Nov 1943	2d Marines participated in Tarawa campaign.
24 Nov 1943	2d Marines redeployed to Camp Tarawa, Hawaii.
15 Jun 1944 to 7 Aug 1944	2d Marines participated in Saipan Campaign and Tinian Campaign.
8 Aug 1944 to Mar 1945	2d Marines performed duty in Saipan.
1 Apr 1945 to 30 Jun 1945	2d Marines participated in Okinawa-Gunto Campaign.

23 Sep 1945 to 13 Jun 1946	2d Marines performed occupation duty in Japan.
12 Jul 1946	2d Marines arrived at Camp Lejeune.
31 Oct 1956 to 3 Nov 1956	Elements of 2d Marines assisted in the evacuation of U.S. observors and other nationals from Alexandria, Egypt.
24 Oct 1962 to 12 Dec 1962	Elements of 2d Marines participated in Cuban Missile Crisis.
1 May 1965 to 29 May 1965	Elements of 2d Marines participated in Dominican Republic Crisis.

APPENDIX E

Honors of the 2d Marines

PRESIDENTIAL UNIT CITATION STREAMER WITH ONE BRONZE STAR
    (Guadalcanal, 7 Aug - 9 Dec 1942)
    (Tarawa, 20-24 Nov 1943)

MEXICAN SERVICE STREAMER
    (21-23 Apr 1914)

HAITIAN CAMPAIGN STREAMER WITH 1915 - 1919 - 1920 CLASP
    (4 Aug 1915 - 6 Dec 1915, 1 Apr 1919 - 15 Jun 1920)

MARINE CORPS EXPEDITIONARY STREAMER WITH ONE BRONZE STAR
    (Haiti, 7 Dec 1915 - 5 Apr 1917, 12 Nov 1918 - 31 Mar 1919,
    16 Jun 1920 - 25 Nov 1924; 4 Dec 1929 - 5 Aug 1931)
    (Cuba, 3-14 Jan, 22 Jan - 16 Mar, 22 Apr - 22 Jun, and
    11 Oct 1961 - 1 Feb 1962)

WORLD WAR I VICTORY STREAMER WITH ONE BRONZE STAR
    (West Indies, 6 Apr 1917 - 11 Nov 1918)

AMERICAN DEFENSE SERVICE STREAMER
    (1 Feb - 7 Dec 1941)

ASIATIC-PACIFIC CAMPAIGN STREAMER WITH ONE SILVER AND ONE BRONZE STAR
    (Guadalcanal-Tulagi Landings, 7-9 Aug 1942)
    (Capture and Defense of Guadalcanal, 10 Aug 1942 - 31 Jan 1943)
    (Gilbert Islands Operation, 20-24 Nov 1943)
    (Capture and Occupation of Saipan, 15 Jun - 24 Jul 1944)
    (Capture and Occupation of Tinian, 24 Jul - 10 Aug 1944)
    (Assault and Occupation of Okinawa Gunto, 1-10 Apr 1945)

WORLD WAR II VICTORY STREAMER
    (7 Dec 1941 - 31 Dec 1946)

NAVY OCCUPATION SERVICE STREAMER WITH ASIA AND EUROPE CLASPS
    (Asia, 23 Sep 1945 - 12 Jun 1946)
    (Europe, 15 Jan - 5 Mar 1943 and various dates through 1950)

NATIONAL DEFENSE SERVICE STREAMER WITH ONE BRONZE STAR
    (27 Jun 1950 - 27 Jul 1954)
    (1 Jan 1961 to date)

ARMED FORCES EXPEDITIONARY STREAMER WITH TWO BRONZE STARS
    (Lebanon, 15 Jul - 13 Aug 1958)
    (Cuba, 24 Oct - 12 Dec 1962)
    (Dominican Republic, 1 - 29 May 1965)

APPENDIX F

2d Marines Medal of Honor Recipients

Maj	Randolph C. Berkeley	21-22 Apr 1914	Vera Cruz, Mexico
Maj	Smedley D. Butler	21-22 Apr 1914	Vera Cruz, Mexico
Capt	Eli T. Fryer	21-22 Apr 1914	Vera Cruz, Mexico
Capt	Walter N. Hill	21-22 Apr 1914	Vera Cruz, Mexico
Capt	John A. Hughes	21-22 Apr 1914	Vera Cruz, Mexico
LtCol	Wendell C. Neville	21-22 Apr 1914	Vera Cruz, Mexico
GySgt	Daniel J. Daly	24 Oct 1915	Ft. Liberte, Haiti
1stLt	Edward A. Ostermann	24 Oct 1915	Ft. Liberte, Haiti
Capt	William P. Upshur	24 Oct 1915	Ft. Liberte, Haiti
1stLt	William D. Hawkins	20-21 Nov 1943	Tarawa, Gilbert Is.
Col	David M. Shoup	20-21 Nov 1943	Tarawa, Gilbert Is.

Made in the USA
Columbia, SC
22 December 2024